RICHARD THE
By Raphael Holinshed

Second sonne to Henrie the second.

An. Reg. 1.
1189.Richard the first of that name, and second sonne of Henrie the second, *Wil. Paruus.*began his reigne ouer England the sixt day of Julie, in the yere of our Lord 1189. in the seauen and thirteeth yeare of the emperour Frederike the first, in the eleuenth yere of the reigne of Philip the second king of France, and king William surnamed the Lion as yet liuing in the gouernement of Scotland.

This Richard, immediatlie after the solemnities of his fathers funerals were ended, made hast to Rouen, where he was ioifullie receiued, and proclamed duke of Normandie, receiuing the inuesture according to the *Matt. Paris.*custome, on the twentith day of Julie. Then studieng to set all things in good order on that side the sea, he made search where his fathers Stephan de Turnham committed to prison.treasure was preserued, and therevpon attached Stephan de Turnham, who was seneschall or gouernour (as we may call him) of Aniou, and committing him to prison, compelled him to make deliuerie of all such summes of monie as he had hid and laid vp in certeine castels by the commandement of the late king his father.

*Matth. Paris. Polydor.*Whilest he was thus occupied, his brother John came to him, to whom he ioifullie gaue the welcome, and besides all other things which his father had bequeathed vnto him by his testament in England, amounting to the value of foure thousand pounds of yearelie rent, with the earledome of Mortaigne, he procured a marriage for him (being now a [203]widower) for Isabell daughter to the earle of Glocester married to John ye kings   brother.
She is named by diuerse authors Hauisia.*Matth. Paris. R. Houed.*his further aduancement with the ladie Isabell, daughter to Robert earle of Glocester, which earle had appointed the said John to be his heire as before is mentioned, although Baldwine the archbishop of Canturburie forbad the mariage, bicause they were coosens in the third degree of consanguinitie. To Robert earle of Leicester also he restored all his lands which had béene taken from him, and such persons as his father had disherited, he restored likewise to their former rights and possessions, howbeit those had forsaken his father, and taken part with him against his said father, he séemed now so much to mislike, that he remooued them vtterlie from his presence, and contrariwise preferred such as had continued faithfull vnto his father in time of the troubles.

*Matt. Paris.*At length, king Richard remembring himselfe of his mother quéene Elianor, who had béene separated from the bed of hir husband for the space of sixtéene yeares, and was as yet deteined in prison in England, wrote his letters vnto the rulers of the realme, commanding them to set The kings mother set at libertie.hir againe at libertie, and withall appointed hir by his letters patents, to take vpon hir the whole gouernment of the kingdome in his absence. The quéene being thus deliuered, and hauing now the cheefe authoritie & rule in hir hands, rode in progresse about the realme, to sée the estate thereof; and as she passed from place to place, she shewed gladsome countenance to the people wheresoeuer she came, dooing also what she could to pleasure them, that she might thereby win their good willes to hir, and to hir sonne: but speciallie remembring by hir late experience and tast thereof, what an irksome & most gréeuous thing imprisonment was, she caused the gailes to be opened, and foorthwith set no small number of prisoners at libertie by the way as she passed through the countries, according to the verse of Virgil,

Non ignara mali miseris succurrere disco.

In the meane time, king Richard concluding a league with Philip king of France, receiued all those places againe which were taken from his father by the same Philip, togither with his wife Adela, whom vpon suspicion that she had beene dishonested in hir person before, without anie sufficient proofe thereof had, he forsooke, & sent hir home with hir dowrie, and otherwise with great and princelie gifts, most bountifullie inriched, hauing alreadie concluded a marriage with the ladie Berengaria, daughter to Garsias king of Nauarre, who was sent into Sicill vnto hir sister Joane, that he might marrie hir there, as he passed that waie towards the holie land.

Whilest these things passed thus in these parties, the christians in The 2. kings of England & France determine to go into the holie landthe holie land dailie sent hither for aid, whereupon the two kings of France and England tooke counsell togither, and determined with all conuenient speed to ioine their powers, & with ships prepared for that purpose to saile into Syria. Hauing thus concluded, they went about to prepare themselues of necessarie prouision for so long a iournie. Now when king Richard had set in order his affaires in Normandie and France, At Southhampton the 21 of August saith *Ger. Dor.Rog. Houed. Matth. Paris.*he came ouer into England, landing at Portesmouth the 13. of August. With him also came his brother John, vnto whom he assigned the castels of Marlebridge, Lutegareshall, Peake, Bollesour, the honor of Wallingford, Tikehill and Eie, with the earledoms of Mortaigne, Dorset, Sumerset, Notingham, Derbie, Deuonshire, and Cornewall, with the earledome of Lancaster, intituling him earle of the same, whereby he was so exalted in state and degree, that he séemed in manner of a tetrarch, hauing as it were a fourth part of the realme in gouernance: but yet the king held some of the castels (in those counties and honors thus giuen to his brother) in his owne hands. Moreouer, vnto William Marshall he gaue in marriage the daughter of Richard earle of Chepstow, togither with the earledome which hir father possessed: and to Gilbert Fitz Roger the sonne of Rainfrey he gaue the daughter of William de Lancaster. After he was landed (as before ye haue heard) he hasted to Winchester, where his mother quéene Elianor with the most part of the English nobilitie had laine a good space to attend his comming, and there on the euen of the assumption of our ladie, the king was by them receiued with great ioy and triumph.

¶ Here is to be noted, that whilest the quéene and lords laie in Winchester waiting for the kings arriuall, Geffrey Riddle the bishop of Elie departed this life. He is named by [204]Geruasius Dorobernensis the proud bishop of Elie: but he might rather haue named him the rich bishop, for he left in his cofers no small quantitie of treasure, of the which thrée thousand and two hundred marks came to the kings part towards the charges of his coronation. No maruell though Geruasius spake somewhat in his dispraise, for (as he himselfe confesseth) he was no fréend but an enimie to moonks.

But to let this passe, soone after the kings comming into England, he was informed that the Welshmen had broken into the English marshes, and destroyed certeine townes; to represse whose presumptuous attempts he made towards them, but was yet staied for that time, & reuoked by his His fathers treasure.mother. At Salisburie he found his fathers treasure, highlie reioising, for that the summe was far greater than he thought it would haue prooued, for besides the pretious stones, apparell, and iewels, it was reported he had there the sum of nine hundred thousand pounds in readie coine. With this good hap king Richard not a little aduanced, came to R. *Houed. Gau. Vinsaf.Nic. Triuet.* The second of September saith *Ger. Dor.*London on the first of September, where he had appointed prouision to be made for his coronation, and so calling a councell of the Nobles of the realme, he receiued the crowne with all due and accustomed solemnitie, at the hands of Baldwin the archbishop of Canturburie, the third daie of September.

The order of his coronatiō.*Matth. Paris.*At his coronation, first the archbishops of Canturburie, Roan, Trier, and Dublin, which were present, with all the other bishops, abbats, and cleargie, apparelled in rich copes, and hauing the crosse, holie water and censures carried afore them, came to fetch him vnto the doore of his priuie chamber, and there receiuing him, they led him vnto the church at Westminster, till he came before the high altar with a solemne *Rog. Houed.*procession. In the middle of the bishops and cleargie went foure barons, bearing candlesticks with tapers, after whom came Geffrey de Lucie bearing the cap of maintenance, and John Marshall next to him, bearing a great and massiue paire of spurs of gold: then followed William Marshall earle of Striguill aliàs Pembroke, who bare the roiall scepter, in the top wherof was set a crosse of gold: and William de Patrike earle of Salisburie going next him, bare the warder or rod, hauing on the top thereof a doue. Then came thrée other earles, Dauid brother to the king of Scots, the earle of Huntington, John the kings brother earle of Mortaigne, and Robert earle of Leicester, ech of them bearing a sword vpright in his hand with the scabberds richlie trimmed and adorned with gold.

The earle of Mortaigne went in the midst betwixt the other two. After *Rog. Houed.*them followed six earles and barons, bearing a checker table, vpon the which was set the kings scochens of armes, and then followed William Mandeuill earle of

Albemarle, bearing a crowne of gold a great heigth before the king, who followed the same, hauing Hugh bishop of Durham on the right hand, and Reignold bishop of Bath on the left, ouer whom a canapie was borne: and in this order he came into the church at Westminster, where before the high altar in the presence of the cleargie & the people, laieng his hand vpon the holie euangelists and the relikes The king his oth.of certeine saincts, he tooke a solemne oth, that he should obserue peace, honour, and reuerence to almightie God, to his church, and to the ministers of the same all the daies of his life. Also that he should exercise vpright iustice to the people committed to his charge, and that he should abrogate and disanull all euill lawes and wrongfull customes, if anie were to be found within the precinct of his realme, and mainteine those that were good and laudable.

This doone, he put off all his garments from the middle vpwards, his shirt excepted which was open on the shoulders, that he might be annointed. The archbishop of Canturburie annointed him then in thrée places, to wit, on the head, on the shoulders, and on the right arme, with praiers in such case accustomed. After this, he couered his head with a linnen cloth hallowed, and set his cap aloft thereon; and then when he had put on his roiall garments and vppermost robe, the archbishop tooke vnto him the sword wherewith he should beat downe the enimies of the church; which doone, two earles put his shoes vpon his feet, and hauing his mantell put on him, the archbishop forbad him on the behalfe of almightie God, not to presume to take vpon him this dignitie [205]except he faithfullie meant to performe those things which he had there sworne to performe. Wherevnto the king made answer, that by Gods grace he would performe them. Then the king tooke the crowne beside the altar, and deliuered it to the archbishop, which he set vpon the kings head, deliuering to him the scepter to hold in his right hand, and the rod roiall in his left hand, & thus being crowned he was brought backe by the bishops and barons, with the crosse and candelsticks, and three swords passing foorth before him vnto his seat. When the bishop that sang the masse came to the offertorie, the two bishops that brought him to the church, led him to the altar, and brought him backe againe.

Finallie when masse was doone, and all things ended in order as was requisit, he was brought with solemne procession into his chamber, where he put off his heauie rich apparell, and put on a crowne and other garments more light and easie, and so went to dinner, whereat wanted no store of meats & drinks, which were serued out in most princelie and bountifull wise.

*Wil. Paruus.*Vpon this daie of king Richards coronation, the Jewes that dwelt in London and in other parts of the realme, being there assembled, had but sorie hap, as it chanced. For they meaning to honour the same coronation The Jewes ment to present him with a rich gift.with their presence, and to present to the king some honourable gift, whereby they might declare themselues glad for his aduancement, and procure his freendship towards them, for the confirming of their priuileges & liberties, according to the grants and charters made to them by the former kings: he of a zealous mind to Christes religion, *Matt. Paris.*abhorring their nation (and doubting some sorcerie by them to be practised) commanded that they should not come within the church when he should receiue the crowne, nor within the palace whilest he was at dinner.

But at dinner time, among other that pressed in at the palace gate, diuerse of the Jewes were about to thrust in, till one of them was A Jew striken.striken by a Christian, who alledging the kings commandement, kept them backe from comming within the palace. Which some of the vnrulie people perceiuing, and supposing it had béene doone by the kings commandement, The people fall vpon the Jewes and beat them.tooke lightlie occasion thereof, and falling vpon the Jewes with staues, bats and stones, beat them and chased them home to their houses and lodgings. Héerewith rose a rumor through the citie, that the king had commanded the Jewes to be destroied, and therevpon came running togither, to assault them in their houses, which when they could not easilie breake vp nor enter, by reason the same were strongly builded, Their houses are set on fire.they set fire on them, so that diuers houses were consumed, not onelie of the Jewes, but also of their neighbours, so hideous was the rage of the fire. Here we see that

  Regis ad exemplum totus componitur orbis.

The king being aduertised of this riotous attempt of the outragious people, sent some of his councellours, as Ranulfe de Glanuille lord Justice, and other officers to appease the tumult: but their authoritie was nothing regarded, nor their persuasions any whit reuerenced, but their thretnings rather brought themselues in danger of life among the rude sort of those that were about to spoile, rob, and sacke the houses and shops of the Jewes: to the better accomplishment of which their vnlawfull act, the light that the fire of those houses which burned, gaue after it was once night, did minister no small helpe and occasion Jewes burnt to death.of furtherance. The Jewes that were in those houses which were set on fire, were either smoldred and burned to death within, or else at their comming foorth most cruellie receiued vpon the points of speares, billes, swords and gleaues of their aduersaries that watched for them verie diligentlie.

This outrage of the furious and disordered people continued from the middest of the one day, till two of the clocke on the other; the commons all that while neuer ceassing their furie against that nation, but still killing them as they met with any of them, in most horrible, rash and vnreasonable maner. At length, rather wearied with their cruell dooings, than satisfied with spoile, or mooued with respect of reason or reuerence of their prince, they withdrew themselues from their riotous enterprise, after they had executed [206]manie vnlawfull and horrible enormities. This great riot well deserued sore and gréeuous punishment, but yet it passed ouer without correction, in respect of the great number of the transgressors, and for that the most part of men for the hatred generallie concerned against the obstinate frowardnesse of the Jewes, liked the dooings hereof well inough, interpreting it to be a good token, that the ioifull daie of the kings aduancement to the crowne should be dolefull vnto the Jewes, in bringing them to such slaughter and destruction. Finallie, after that the tumult was ceassed, the king commanded that no man should hurt or harme any of the Jewes, and so they were restored to peace, after they had susteined infinit damage

¶ The occasion of this tragedie and bloudie tumult (redounding to the Jewes great vexation and pitifull distresse, but to the satisfieng of the peoples furious and vnbridled pronesse to crueltie) sprang principallie from the king, who if he had not so lightlie esteemed of the Jewes when they repaired vnto him with their present, in signe of submission and hope of obteining their sute then purposed to be exhibited; this hurlie burlie had not insued. For it was a violent example & a mightie motiue to the people to maligne the Jewes; as also a hart-gréefe to them in respect of their reiection, when the prince gaue them so discourteous a repulse. Here therefore is to be obserued, that the people is the princes ape, as one verie well saith. For looke whereto he is inclined, note wherein he delighteth; the same is the practise of the people: in consideration whereof the mightie ones of the world haue speciall cause to haue an eie to their course of life, & to set caueats before their actions, that the people may in them sée none but good signes of commendable & vertuous imitation. For

Pal. in suo sag.────── regis imagoVulgus, & ad mores accedere principis optat.Qualis enim rex est talis quoque subditus illiEsse solet populus, studijsque tenetur ijsdem.

A councell at Pipewell.Shortlie after, to wit, the 15. day of September, a councell was holden at Pipewell, where the bishops and abbats being assembled, there were in presence of the king and of the archbishop of Canturburie elected certeine bishops and abbats to such places as then were vacant: and amongst other, William de Longchampe the kings chancellor was elected to *Wil. Paruus.*the sée of Elie, Geffrey the kings bastard brother vnto the archbishoprike of Yorke, who was the 32. in number that had gouerned the same, Geffrey de Lucie to Winchester, one Hubert Walter to Salisburie, and Richard archdeacon of Elie, and the kings treasurer to the see of London. The abbeies that were prouided of abbats were these, Glastenburie, Shirborne, Persore and Feuersham. In like manner, John the The bishop of Whitherne consecrated. *Rog. Houed.*elect of Whitherne was consecrated bishop of that see, by the hands of the archbishop of Dublin. Also in this councell the king ordeined Hugh bishop of Durham, and William Mandeuille earle of Albemarle, lord chéefe iustices of England, hauing deposed Ranulfe de Glanuille from that roome.

Moreouer, the king being thus established in the estate of the kingdome, did not forget his iournie which he had promised into the holie land, but with all diligence made his prouision, and namelie he sought to gather monie to furnish his charges, and so therevpon leuied a tax, engaged, sold, and let to farme his lands, tols, customs, and other his *Matt. Par.*reuenewes, with certeine counties and offices, so that he made an exceeding summe of monie. He also found, that Ranulfe de Glanuille lord chéefe iustice, and other of the head magistrates had not behaued themselues vprightlie in the administration of their offices; so that he both deposed the said lord cheefe iustice as is aforesaid, and almost all the shiriffes and their deputies within the realme of England, putting them to greeuous fines for their offenses and transgressions, and so by that meanes he got no small deale of monie.

Wil. Paruus.¶ Here note by the waie, how William Paruus affirmeth, that where this Ranulfe Glanuille, being a man of high wisedome and stept into age, saw that, manie things were doone [207]by the new king, not so aduisedlie, nor with such foresight as they ought to be, sought of his owne accord to be discharged of his office, that he might the better prepare himselfe to go in that iournie to the holie land, as by taking vpon him the crosse he had vowed in the daies of king Henrie, and so he solemnelie renounced his office, which other (nothing so worthie of it) did afterwards inioy.

Moreouer, the king vnderstanding that Hugh Putsey or Pudsey bishop of Durham, being a verie aged man, had much monie, he sold to him the manour of Seggesfield or Sadberge, with the wapentake belonging to the same, and also found meanes to persuade him to buy his owne prouince, which he did, giuing to the king an inestimable summe of monie, and was The bishop of Durham Sadberge. The bishop of Durham made an earle.therevpon created an earle by the king for the same: wherevpon he was intituled both bishop and earle of Durham, whereat the king would iest afterwards and saie; "What a cunning craftesman am I, that haue made a new earle of an old bishop?"

Furthermore, the same bishop gaue to the king a thousand markes to be made chéefe iustice of England, and that he might tarrie at home, and not go into the holie land. And bicause he would not be reprooued of any person, he obteined of the apostolike sée (which faileth no man that is surcharged with white or red mettall, and would be eased) a licence for a summe of monie to be dispensed with for that iournie. The king thus being earnestlie bent to make commoditie of those things, for the which The citizens of London present monie to the King.
Polydor.
Liberties granted to London. Two bailiffes.he might get any monie at all, the citizens of London presented vnto him a great summe towards the furnishing foorth of his enterprise. Wherevpon to acquite their courtesie, he granted them large priuileges, and ordeined that the citie should be ruled by two head officers, which they should choose amongst themselues remoueable from yeare to yeare by the name of bailiffes. The names of the two first bailiffes chosen by force of that ordinance, were[1], Henrie Cornehill, and Richard Fitz Reiner.

The citie before those daies euer since the comming in of William Conquerour, and a good while before his time, was gouerned by certeine Port Greues.officers or rulers named Port Greues (which word is deriued of two Saxon words, as Port and Greue. By Port is meant a towne, and by Greue a gardian or ruler, as who should saie, A kéeper or ruler of a towne.) These rulers with[2] the lawes & customes then vsed within this citie, were registered in a booke called (as some haue said) Doomesdaie, but through negligence after these lawes and customes were changed and altered, the booke was lost, so that the remembrance of such rulers as were before the daies of this Richard the first are not to be had. These bailiffes euer entred at Michaelmasse, and so continued foorth their yeare.

Thus began the citie first to receiue the forme and state of a common-wealth, and to be diuided into felowships, which they call crafts or corporations. Such also are admitted to the fellowships of these Apprentises.companies, as haue truelie serued as apprentises a certeine number of yeares, as seuen at the least, vnder which time of seruice expired, there is none made frée, nor suffered to inioy the liberties of that Fréemen.citie, sauing such as are borne free, that is to saie, of fréemen within the citie, of whome at this time, it is not much materiall to make any further report. The citie thus consisting of the said craftes or occupations, chooseth out of the same a senat or companie of graue councellours, whom they name Aldermen (E) changed into (A) according to Wards.the old Saxon pronuntiation. It is also diuided into 26. tribes or wards, of the which euerie one hath his seuerall Alderman, or ouerseer, who haue both authoritie sufficient, and large priuileges to mainteine the good gouernement of their portions withall. Out of the number of these, there is another officer yearelie chosen and appointed, called The Maior.the Maior, who ruleth all the rest.

But now to returne vnto the further dooings of king Richard before his departure out of England towards his iournie into the land of Palestine, commonlie called Holie land, it is said, he made such sale of things apperteining to him, as well in right of the crowne, [208]as otherwise, that it séemed to diuerse he made his reckoning neuer to returne againe, in so much that some of his councellours told him plainelie, that he did K. Richard setteth things on sale. *Ran. Higd.Wil. Paruus.*not well in making things awaie so fréelie, to the dishonoring of his maiestie, and preiudice of his successour; vnto whome he answered, "that in time of need it was no euill policie for a man to help himselfe with his owne," and further ioined hereto these words, "that if London at that time of néed would be bought, he would surelie sell it, if he might méet with a conuenient merchant that were able to giue him monie inough for it."

Another way he had also to gather riches, and that was this. He had a licence of pope Innocent the third, to dispense with such as pleased him within his realme, for their vowes made to go into the holie land, although they had taken on them the crosse for that purpose, namelie such as he should appoint to remaine behind him for the defense of his countrie: and of these also he tooke abundantlie, and diuerse other he compelled to fine, namelie, to the end that he might get their monie likewise, that hereby he obteined no small summe toward the furniture of his iournie. But both pope & prince forgat in the meane while, that

Boni pastoris est tondere pecus non excoriare.

This yeare also in the moneth of Nouember, as Matthew Paris saith, Johannes de Anagnia a cardinall and legat from the pope arriued here in England, comming on land at Douer, and bicause the king was as then in the north parts, the same cardinall was prohibited on the behalfe of the kings mother quéene Elianor, to passe any further without the kings commandement. And so he staied there thirtéene daies at the charges of the archbishop of Canturburie, till the king came to those parties, by whose wisedome a direction was taken for the quieting of the controuersie betwixt the archbishop, and the moonkes of Canturburie, for the chappell church of Hakington now called S. Stephans.

*R. Houed.*In the same moneth of Nouember, by the kings appointment, Geffrey the elect of Yorke, who was the kings brother, with other barons and lords William king of Scots.of Yorkeshire, receiued William king of Scotland at the water of Tweed, and from thence with all due reuerence and honour they brought him vnto A councell called at Canturburie.

Polydor.
An oth.
*Matth. Paris.*Canturburie, where the king had called a councell of the lords of his realme both spirituall and temporall, in the which euerie of them tooke an oth to be true to the king, and to continue in due obedience vnder him and his lawes, which oth also the king of Scots receiued, being there present, and likewise king Richards brethren earle John and Geffrey the archbishop of Yorke.

*Matth. Paris. Polydor.*The king of Scots therefore hauing receiued this oth, and thinking the time to serue his purpose for redéeming of those castels, which were deliuered to king Henrie as gages for his ransome, paid now vnto king Restitution made to the K. of Scots. *Wil. Paruus.*Richard ten thousand markes, and had restitution for the same, that is of Berwike, Roxburgh, Sterling, and Edenburgh. But William Paruus saieth, that Edenburgh was restored to him in the daies of king Henrie, by reason of his wife which he tooke in the parties beyond the seas: and herewith agréeth the Scotish chronicle. King Richard also assigned to queene Elianor his mother, the accustomed dower, with manie lordships *Rog. Houed.*and honours beside, as an augmentation thereof. About which time died William de Mandeuille earle of Albemarle at Rouen, and Hugh de Putsey *N. Triuet.*the nephue of the bishop of Durham died at Aclet, and was buried at Durham. Also Formalis archbishop of Trier died at Northampton, and was there buried in the church of S. Andrews.

In the meane time, king Richard still desirous to furnish himselfe with monie, deuised yet another shift, and feigned that he had lost his seale; wherefore he commanded a new to be made, which being doone, he *Matth. Paris.*caused it to be proclaimed and published in euerie countrie, that those to whome he had granted any thing by his déed or charter, meaning to inioy the same in suretie, should not thinke it much to come and haue it confirmed by his new seale, least afterward the other being lost, their lawfull titles might be called into question. Wherevpon manie that could not come to him whilest he was in England, [209]were glad to follow him, and saile ouer into Normandie, and there to fine at his pleasure for the new seale, to the end that their writings might be confirmed thereby, and made so much the more sure to them and their successours. For the same businesse also Remigius the prior of S. Albons, and manie other went ouer to their great costs, charges, and trauell, after he was transported into France.

I find moreouer about the same time, that the kings brother earle John exhibited a sore complaint against the Romane legat and other bishops, for that the archbishop of Canturburie, after the appeale made vnto the apostolike sea, had put his lands vnder interdiction for his mariage made with the earle of Glocesters daughter: which when the legat heard, he foorthwith confirmed the appeale, and released the earles lands of the aforesaid interdiction. The same time also, the tenth part of all the mooueable goods thorough the realme of England was leuied to the aid of the warres in the holie land. And this collection passing vnder the name of an almes, was extended vpon the goods as well of the spirituall men as temporall.

After all this, K. Richard desirous to set order in the gouernment of Hugh bishop of Durham gouerneth the north parts.*Matth. Paris.*his realme, appointed Hugh bishop of Durham to haue the rule of the north parts as cheefe iustice from Humber northwards toward Scotland, deliuering vnto him also the keeping of Winchester castell: the residue of the kingdome (with the custodie of the towre) he assigned to the William Lōgchampe bishop of Elie.gouernance of William Longchampe bishop of Elie, whome he had made cheefe iustice of that part, and chancellour of the realme, a man of great diligence and knowledge in the administration of things, but verie factious and desirous of rule, honour and riches farre aboue all measure. And with these two he ioined in commission Hugh Bardulfe, William Marshall earle of Chepstow, or rather Penbrooke, Geffrey Fitz-Peter, & William Brewer, men of great honour, wisedome, and discretion.

R. *Houed.* King Richard passeth ouer in to Normandie.On the fift day of December, he departed from Canturburie, and went to Douer, there to take water, and so on the eleuenth day of December he passed ouer vnto Calice, where he found Philip earle of Flanders readie to recciue him, who attended vpon him till he came into Normandie, where 1190.the king held his Christmas at Burun, and immediatlie came to an enteruiew with the French king at Gue S. Remige, where they concluded *Vadum sancti Remigij.* A league betwixt yᵉ kings of England and France.peace togither, to be kept betwixt them & their countries on ech part; the which was put in writing, and confirmed with their oths and seales in the feast of saint Hilarie.

R. *Houed.*Furthermore, about the purification of our ladie, Elianor the quéene mother, and the ladie Alice sister to the French king, Baldwine archbishop of Canturburie, John bishop of Norwhich, Hugh bishop of Durham, Geffrey bishop of Winchester, Reignold bishop of Bath, William Bishop of Elie, Hubert bishop of Salisburie, and Hugh bishop of Chester, with Geffrey the elect of Yorke and John earle of Mortaigne the kings two brethren, by commandement of the king passed ouer into Normandie, to commen with him before his setting forward.

¶ Some write, that now at this present, the king should ordeine or rather confirme the bishop of Elie his chancellour to be lord chéefe iustice ouer all England, and the bishop of Durham to be lord iustice Contention betwixt two ambitious bishops.from Trent northwards. But whensoeuer they were thus aduanced to such dignities, howsoeuer they came by them, directlie or indirectlie, true it is, that immediatlie therevpon, strife and discord did arise betwixt them: for waxing proud and insolent, they disdained ech other, contending which of them should bare most rule and authoritie, insomuch that whatsoeuer séemed good to the one, the other misliked, as in cases where[3] parteners in authoritie are equall, it often happeneth. The like hereof is noted before betwéene the archbishops of Canturburie and Yorke in diuerse kings reignes. For the nature of ambition is to delight in singularitie, to admit no peere, to giue place to no superior, to acknowledge no equall. Hereto alludeth the poet verie neatlie, and exemplifieth it in the old Romans, the order of whose actions is [210]continued at this day, as by the words insuing may be gathered, and ordinarilie obserued booth here and elsewhere;

M. Pal. in sua virg.—— olimRomulidæ orabant, iacto post terga pudorePlebeios, quoties suffragia venabantur,Cerdonúmq; animos precibus seruilibus atq;Turpibus obsequijs captabant, muneribúsq;Vt proprijs rebus curarent publica omissis;Pérq; forum medium multis comitantibus irent,Inflati vt vento folles, ac fronte superba, &c.

Moreouer, at the same time he caused his two brethren, earle John, and Geffrey the elect archbishop of Yorke to take an oth not to returne into England during the terme of thrée yeares next insuing, without his consent and licence first had. This he did, foreséeing what might happen, prouiding as it were against such practises as his brethren might happilie attempt against him. But yet his mother quéene Elianor procured him to reuoke that decree immediatlie, least it might seeme to the world, that hir sonnes should stand in feare one of another. And so Erle John licenced to returne into England.the earle of Mortaigne was licenced to returne into England at his pleasure, swearing an oth at his departure to obeie the kings beheast, and truelie to serue him, according to the dutie of a good and loiall subiect. The bishop of Elie lord chancellour and cheefe iustice of England was also sent backe hither into this realme, to set forward things behoouefull for the kings iournie.

The bishop of Elie returneth.In like maner the king sent to Rome to obteine that the said bishop of Elie might be constituted the popes legat through both the prouinces of Canturburie and Yorke, and likewise through Wales and Ireland. Which was soone granted by the bulles of pope Clement the third, bearing date the 5. of June. For the which office the bishops gaue him 1500. marks, to the great offense of the king, as he shewed afterward to cardinall Octauian that came to visit him when he arriued in the riuer of Tiber, being vpon his iourneie towards Messina, as after may appeare. But in the meanetime, calling togither the lords, and peeres of those his *Polydor.*dominions on that side the sea, to wit, Normandie, Britaine, Aniou, Poitou, and Guien, he consulted with them what number of soldiors and how many ships it should be conuenient for him to take with him and furnish into Asia: and herewith he did command them also to obeie Robert earle of Leicester, whome he appointed to remaine amongst them as his lieutenant or vicegerent of those parts during his absence.

¶ But here to leaue king Richard in consultation for matters appertaining to his iournie, and shew brieflie what happened (by the *W. Paruus.*waie) to the Jewes, which as then dwelt heere in England, after that king Richard was passed ouer into Normandie: ye haue heard how after the riot against them at London, when the king was crowned, he tooke order that they should remaine in peace vnder his protection, and commanded that no person should in anie wise molest them. But now after that he was gone ouer, and that the souldiers (which prepared themselues to follow him) began to assemble in routs, the heads of the common people began to wax wild and faine would they haue had some occasion of raising The hatred borne to the Jewes.a new tumult against the Jewes, whome (for their vnmercifull vsurie practised to the vndooing of manie an honest man) they most deadlie hated, wishing most earnestlie their expulsion out of England. Hervpon by reason of a riot committed latelie against them, at the towne of Lin in Norfolke, where manie of them were slaine, other people in other parts of the realme, taking occasion hereat, as if they had béene called vp by the sound of a bell or trumpet, arose against them in those townes where they had any habitations, and robbed and bet them after a disordered and most riotous maner.

*Iohn Textor.*As at Stamford (on the faire day in Lent); at Lincolne and at Yorke, in which citie [211]after a number of them had béene besieged certeine daies within a towre of the kings (whither they fled for succour) one of their Fiue hundred saith *Houeden*and *Textor.*learned gouernours caused foure hundred of their companie to consent to haue their throts cut one at an others hands, he himselfe cutting his wiues throt first, whose name was Anna, then his childrens, one after another, and last of all slue himselfe onelie rather than he would fall into the hands of the christians, that had thus long besieged them. The rest perceiuing what their great Rabbi had doone, set fire vpon all their goods and substance, which they had gotten into the tower with them, and so consuming the same, would haue burnt also the residue of their fellowes which would not agrée to the

Rabbies counsell, in the cruell murthering of themselues, if they had not taken a strong turret hard by within that tower, and defended themselues both from the fire and crueltie of their brethren, who had made awaie themselues in such manner as I haue said: and that to the number of foure hundred, or (as some write) fiue hundred at the least.

On the morow, those that were saued, called out to the people, and not onelie shewed how and after what sort their fellowes were dispatched, but also offered to be baptised, and forsake their Judaisme, if they might haue their liues saued from the imminent & present danger wherein they saw themselues to be wrapped, through the furie of the people. To be short, this thing was granted, and they came foorth, howbeit they were no sooner entred into the prease, but they were all slaine, and not one man of them preserued.

After this also, the people ran to the cathedrall church, and broke into those places where their bonds and obligations laie, by the which they had diuerse of the kings subiects bound vnto them in most vnconscionable sort, and for such detestable vsurie as (if the authors that write thereof were not of credit) would hardlie be beleeued. All which euidences or bonds they solemnelie burned in the middest of the church. After which, ech went his waie, the souldiers to the king, and the commons to their houses, and so was the citie quieted. This happened at Yorke on Palmesundaie eeue, being the 17. of March: and vpon the 15. of that moneth, those that inhabited in the towne of S. Edmundsburie in Suffolke, were set vpon, and manie of them slaine. The residue that escaped, through the procurement of the abbat then named Samson, were expelled, so that they neuer had anie dwellings there since that time.

Thus were the Jewes vnmercifullie dealt with in all places in maner through this realme, the first beginning whereof chanced at London (as before ye haue heard) and the next at Lin, of which I thinke it good to note some part of the maner therof, although breeflie, and so to returne to my purpose. The occasion therefore of the tumult at Lin chanced by this meanes: it fortuned that one of the Jewes there was become a christian, wherewith those of his nation were so mooued, that they determined to kill him where soeuer they might find him. And herevpon they set vpon him one daie as he came by, through the streets: he to escape their hands fled to the next church; but his countriemen were so desirous to execute their malicious purpose, that they followed him still, and inforced themselues to breake into the church vpon him. Herewith the noise being raised by the christians that sought to saue the conuerted Jew, a number of mariners being forreners, that were arriued there with their vessells out of sundrie parts, and diuerse also of the townesmen came to the rescue, and setting vpon the Jewes, caused them to flee into their houses.

The townesmen were not verie earnest in pursuing of them, bicause of the kings proclamation and ordinance before time made in fauour of the The slaughter made of the Jews at Lin.Jewes: but the mariners followed them to their houses, slue diuerse of them, robbed and sacked their goods, and finallie set their dwellings on fire, and so burnt them vp altogither. These mariners being inriched with the spoile of the Jewes goods, and fearing to be called to accompt for their vnlawfull act by the kings officers, got them foorthwith to shipboord, and hoising vp sailes, departed with their ships to the sea, and so escaped the danger of that [212]which might haue béene otherwise laid to their charge. The townesmen being called to an accompt excused themselues by the mariners, burdening them with all the fault. But although they of Lin were thus excused, yet they of Yorke escaped not so easilie. For the king being aduertised of such outrage, doone contrarie to the order of his lawes and expresse commandement, wrote ouer to the bishop of Elie his chancellour, charging him to take cruell punishment of the offenders.

The bishop with an armie went to Yorke, but the cheefe authors of the riot hearing of his comming, fled into Scotland: yet the bishop at his comming to the citie, caused earnest inquirie to be made of the whole matter. The citizens excused themselues, & offered to proue that they were not of counsel with them that had committed the riot, neither had they aided nor comforted them therein an anie maner of wise. And in déed the most part of them that were the offenders, were of the countries and townes néere to the citie, with such as were crossed into the holie land, and now gone ouer to the king, so that verie few or none of the substantiall men of the citie were found to haue ioined with them. The citizens of Yorke put to their fine for slaughter of the Jewes. Howbeit this would not excuse the citizens, but that they were put to their fine by the stout Bishop, euerie of them paieng his portion according to his power and abilitie in substance, the common sort of the poore people being pardoned, and not called into iudgement, sith the ringleaders were fled and gone out of the waie: and thus much by waie of digression touching the Jews.

Now to returne vnto the king, who in this meane time was verie busie to prouide all things necessarie to set forward on his iournie; his ships which laie in the mouth of the riuer of Saine, being readie to put off, he tooke order in manie points concerning the state of the common-wealth on that side, and chéefelie he called to mind, that it should be a thing necessarie for him, to name who should succeed him in the kingdome of England, if his chance should not be to returne againe from so long and *Matt. West.*dangerous a iournie. He therefore named (as some suppose) his nephue Arthur, the sonne of his brother Geffrey duke of Britaine, to be his successour in the kingdome, a yoong man of a likelie proofe and princelie towardnesse, but not ordeined by God to succéed ouer this kingdome.

About the same time the bishop of Elie, lord chancellour and cheefe iustice of England, tooke vp to the kings vse, of euerie citie in England two palfries and two sumpter horsses, & of euerie abbeie one palfrie and one sumpter horsse, & euerie manour within the realme found also one palfrie and one sumpter horsse. Moreouer, the said bishop of Elie, deliuered the gouernement of Yorkeshire to his brother Osbert de Longchampe: and all those knights of the said shire, the which would not come to make answer to the law vpon summons giuen them, he commanded to be apprehended and by and by cast in prison. Also when the bishop of Durham was returned from the king and come ouer into England to go vnto his charge, at his meeting with the lord chancellour at Elie (notwithstanding that he shewed him his letters patents of the grant made to him to be iustice from Trent northward) the said lord The bishop of Durham restreined of libertie.chancellour taking his iournie to Southwell with him, there deteined him as prisoner, till he had made surrender to him of the castell of Windsor, & further had deliuered to him his sonnes, Henrie de Putsey, and Gilbert de la Ley, as pledges that he should keepe the peace against the king and all his subiects, vntill the said prince should returne from the holie land. And so he was deliuered for that time, though shortlie after, and whilest he remained at Houeden, there came to him Osbert de Longchampe the lord chancellours brother, and William de Stuteuille, the which caused the said bishop to find sufficient suretie that he should not thence depart without the kings licence, or the lord chancellors, so long as the king should be absent. Herevpon the bishop of Durham sent knowledge to the king how and in what sort he had béene handled by the chancellor.

In the meane time the king was gone into Gascoigne, where he besieged a William de Chisi.castell that belonged to one William de Chisi, and tooke both the castell and the owner, whome he [213]caused to be hanged for the spoiles and robberies which he had committed vpon pilgrims that passed by those parts toward Compostella, to visit the bodie of saint James. After this, the king came backe vnto Chinon in Aniou, and there tooke order for the The kings nauie is set foorth. Baion.
Sablius, or Sabuille.setting foorth of his nauie by sea, ouer which he appointed chéefe gouernours Gerard archbishop of Aux, Bernard bishop of Baieux, Robert de Sablius, Richard de Camuille[4], and William de Fortz de Vlerun, commanding all those that should passe foorth with his said nauie, to be obedient vnto these persons as his deputies and lieutenants. Herewith they were appointed to prouide victuals to serue all those that should go by sea for the space of 60 daies.

*Polydor.*The king also made the same time certeine ordinances to be obserued among the seafaring men which tended to this effect:

Slaiers of men.1 First, that if any man chanced to slea an other on the shipboord, he should be bound to the dead bodie and so throwne into the sea.

2 Secondlie, if he killed him on land, he should yet be bound to him as before, and so buried quicke togither.

Brallers. Punishment for blouddrawers.3 Thirdlie, if any man should be conuicted by lawfull witnesse, that he drew any weapon to strike any other, or chanced by striking at any man to draw bloud of him that was smitten, he should lose his hand.

4 Fourthlie, if he gaue but a blowe with his fist without bloudshedding, he should be plunged three seuerall times ouer head and eares in the water.

Reuilers.5 Fifthlie, if any man reuiled another, he should for euerie time so misusing himselfe, forfeit an ounce of siluer.

Theft and pickeries.6 Sixtlie, that if anie man were taken with theft or pickerie, and thereof conuicted, he should haue his head polled, and hot pitch powred vpon his pate, and vpon that, the feathers of some pillow or cushion shaken aloft, that he might thereby be knowne for a theefe, and at the next arriuall of the ships to any land, be put foorth of the companie to seeke his aduenture, without all hope of returne vnto his fellowes.

These were the statutes which this famous prince did enact at the first for his nauie, which sithens that time haue been verie much inlarged. About the same time John Bishop of Whiterne in Scotland, suffragane to the church of Yorke, ordeined Geffrey archbishop of Yorke, préest. At *Wil. Paruus*.the same season also the election of the same Geffrey was confirmed by pope Clement, who among other things that he wrote to the chapiter of Yorke on his behalfe, in the end he addeth these words: "We do therefore admonish you all, and by the apostolicall bulles command you, that you exhibit both reuerence and honour vnto him as vnto your prelat, that thereby you may appeare commendable both before God and man. Giuen at Lateran in the nones of March and third yeare of our gouernment."

Whilest these things were in dooing, there came into France legats from the said Clement, to mooue the two kings to make all the spéed possible towards their iourneie, bicause of the great danger wherein things stood in Palestine, requiring present helpe. Herevpon king Richard (his men and prouision being readie) commanded that his ships should set forward, & to coast about by the streicts of Giberalterre to come vnto *Polydor*. King Richard set forward on his iournie.*Rog. Houed.*Marseilles, where he appointed to méet them, and so with a chosen companie of men he also set foorth thitherwards by land, and comming to Tours, receiued the scrip and staffe as a pilgrime should, at the hands of the archbishop there.

After this, both the kings of England and France met at Vizeley in the octaues of the natiuitie of S. John Baptist, and when they had remained there two daies they passed foorth to the citie of Lion; where the two kings departed in sunder, and each one kept his iournie, the one toward An. Reg. 2.Guenes, where his nauie was appointed to come to him, and the other to Marseilles, there to méet with his fléet, according to his appointment. The English fléet staied by contrarie winds.But the English ships being let and staied by the way by contrarie winds and rigorous tempests, which tossed them[5] to and fro vpon the coasts of Spaine, could not come in [214]any conuenient time vnto Marseilles, so that king Richard thinking long to tarrie for them, & perceiuing they could Twentie gallies & twelue other vessels saith *Houed.*Vpon the seauenth day of August saith *Houeden.*not kéepe their appointed time, he hired ships from all places thereabouts, and embarking himselfe and his men in the same, vpon saint Laurence euen, sailed foorth towards Sicile, where he was appointed to méet with king Philip.

*Rog. Houed.*Here is to be noted, that king Richard made not all that iourneie from Marseilles to Messina by sea, but sundrie times comming on land, hired horsses, and rode foorth alongst the coast, appointing with his ships and gallies where to meet him, and sometimes he rested certeine daies togither in one place or other as at Portdelphin, at Naples, and at Salerne, from whence there departed from him Baldwine archbishop of Canturburie, Hubert bishop of Salisburie, and the lord Ranulfe de Glanuille, the which taking vpon them to go before, with prosperous wind and weather in short space landed at Acon, which was then besieged, as you shall heare hereafter.

At Rome the king came not, but being within the streame of the riuer of Tiber, there came to him a cardinall named Octauianus, bishop of Hostia, King Richard blameth the court of Rome for couetousnesse.to whome be spake manie reprochfull words of the couetousnesse vsed in the court of Rome (a vice reputed the common nursse of all mischéefes, as one verie well noteth,

11

Vbi auaritia est, habitant fermè omnia ibidemFlagitia, impietas, periuria, furta, rapinæ,Fraudes atq; doli, insidiæq; & proditiones,Iurgia & infandæ cædes, &c.)

Bicause they had receiued seauen hundred marks for the consecration of the bishop of Mauns, and 1500. marks for the confirming of the bishop of Elie the popes legat. And againe no small summe of monie they had receiued of the archbishop of Burdeaux, when vpon an accusation brought against him by the cleargie of his prouince he should haue béene deposed. In the meane time whiles king Richard thus passed forward towards Messina, the nauie that was appointed to coast about Spaine and to méet him at Marseilles, was tossed (as before is said) with wind and tempests, and a part thereof, that is, to wit, ten ships driuen here and there on the coasts of Spaine, of which number nine arriued at Lisbone and the tenth being a ship of London arriued at the citie of Sylua, which was then the vttermost citie of Spaine, that was inhabited with christians.

The Saracens at that time made warres against the king of Portingale, so that the Portingales stood in néed of aid, in so much that they of Sylua did not onelie intreat the Englishmen to staie with them for a time, but also got grant of them to breake their ship, with the timber whereof they might the better fortifie their towne, promising that their king should recompense them with an other as good as theirs, and also further satisfie them for their seruice, during the time of their abode therein defense of that citie. Likewise of those that arriued at Lisbone there went to the number of fiue hundred vnto saint Iranes, where the king of The king of Portingale.Portingale then was, looking to be assaulted by his enimies: but by the counterfet[6] death of the great K. of the Saracens named Boiac Almiramumoli king of the Saracens.Almiramumoli (who feared these new succours, and doubted the sequele of his dooings, to the end he might depart with honour, he fained himselfe dead) the king of Portingale was for that time presentlie deliuered out of danger.

Herevpon he returned to Lisbone, where he found thrée score and thrée other ships of king Richards nauie there newlie arriued, ouer the which Robert de Sabuuille. Richard de Camuille.were chéefe capteins Robert de Sabuuille, and Richard de Camuille: which at their comming to land could not so gouerne their people, but that some naughtie fellowes amongst them fell to breaking and robbing of orchards: some also entring into the citie, behaued themselues verie disorderlie. But yet by the comming of the king, their lewdnesse was staied; so that he seemed not to séeke reuenge of the pilgrims, but rather with courteous meanes to bridle their vnlawfull attempts: wherevnto the diligence of the English capteines not a little preuailed [215]for a while, but yet for all that could be done on both sides, within three daies after, a new tumult was raised betwixt the English pilgrims and the townesmen, and diuerse hurt and killed on either part.

A mutinie betwixt the Englishmen and the townsmen of Lisbone. Englishmen committed to prison.Wherevpon the king caused the gates of the citie to be shut, and all those that were come from the ships into the citie to eat and drinke (being in number about seauen hundred) were apprehended and committed to ward: and before they could be released, sir Robert Sabuuille and sir Richard Camuille were glad to agree with the king, so as all former offenses being remitted, and things taken by either part restored, the Englishmen promised to obserue the peace against the king of Portingale and his people; and he likewise couenanted for him and his subiects, that they should kéepe the peace against all pilgrims that went foorth in this voiage, and vse them like his fréends, and thus the quarell ceased.

Soone after, the English nauie departed from Lisbone, and came into the mouth of the riuer of Taie, betwéene Caperico and Belem, where the same daie on saint James éeue the lord William de Forzdulerun arriued also with thrée and thirtie other ships, and so then they were in all about The English ships méet togither.an hundred and six sailes verie well furnished and manned, and so from thence taking their course towards Marseilles, finallie they arriued there in the octaues of the assumption of our ladie; and staieng there an eight daies (till they had repaired such things about their ships as were néedfull) they set forward againe, and came to Messina in Sicile in the feast of the exaltation of the crosse. On the sunday following also came the French king thither, hauing lost no small part of his nauie by tempests of weather.

They arriue at Messina.King Richard as then remained at Salern, and hearing that his nauie was gone towards Messina, he departed thence on the thirteenth day of September, and hasted forth towards Messina, passing by Melphi and Cocenza, and so at length comming to Faro de Messina, he passed the K. Richard arriueth at Messina.same, and on the 23. day of September arriued at Messina with great noise of trumpets and other instruments, to the woonder of the French king and others that beheld his great puissance and roiall behauiour now at this comming. The same time he went vnto the French kings lodging, to commen with him of their businesse: and immediatlie the French king tooke the sea, in purpose to haue passed forward on his iournie but by contrarie wind he was staied and kept backe within the hauen, wherevpon both the kings determined to winter there, and in the meane time to prouide themselues of alle things necessarie for their iournie, against the beginning of the next spring. On the 30. of September he receiued his sister the quéene of Sicile, the widow of William the late king of that Ile, whom he placed in a strong fortresse, which he tooke the same day and left therein a conuenient garison of men of armes and demilances for the safegard of the place and of his said sister.

¶ But now for the better vnderstanding of the cause of such quarelling as fell out betwixt the Englishmen and the Sicilians, yée shall vnderstand that a little before the arriuall of the kings of England and France in those parts, king William of Sicile was departed this life, leauing no issue behind him. Wherevpon the lords of the Ile elected one Tancred to their king, a bastard sonne of Roger sometime king of that land, and grandfather to this last decessed king William. This Tancred though he receiued king Richard verie courteouslie; yet he greatlie trusted him not, bicause he demanded the dowrie of his sister quéene Ioane, wife to the late king William to be restored, whereas he had not readie monie to discharge it.

A chaire of gold.Furthermore to depart with the citie of Mount saint Angelo; with all the countrie therevnto belonging; which was indéed assigned to hir for hir dowrie, he thought in no wise profitable: but king Richard did not K. Richards demands for the dowrie of his sister wife to K. William.onelie require that citie and countie with a chaire of gold, according to the custome of that kingdome in right of his sister, as due to hir by way of hir dowrie, but also he required to his owne vse a table of gold conteining twelue foot in length, and one foot and a halfe in breadth, & two tressels of gold to [216]beare vp the same table, with 24. siluer cups, and as manie dishes of siluer, with a tent of silke of such largenesse that two hundred knights might sit at meat within it: also fortie thousand measures of wheat, with as manie of barlie, and as manie of wine, beside one hundred armed gallies, with all furniture and vittels sufficient to serue the gallie-men in the same for the terme of two yeares. These things he demanded as due to him being heire to his father king Henrie, accordinglie as was deuised by king William in his last will and testament, which demands seemed intollerable to the said Tancred: so that if he could haue shifted the matter, he was loth to haue heard thereof.

Moreouer, bicause pope Clement in right of the church pretended a title to the realme of Sicile, now that king William was dead without heires, he doubted of some practise that might be made against him betwixt king Richard and the pope. Wherevpon he thought to prouide against all attempts that might be made, fortifieng his townes & castels with strong garisons, and tooke counsell with the citizens of Messina, by what meanes he might soonest dispatch his countrie of that present danger, and procure K. Richard to get him forward on his iournie.

Whilest these things were in hand, there was ministred to the English men occasion of displeasure: for as it oftentimes chanceth (where an armie is) certeine of the vnrulie souldiers within Messina vsed themselues somewhat riotouslie, wherevpon the citizens offended therewith, got them to armour, and chased all the souldiers out of the citie. King Richard who laie in campe without the walles néere to the citie, was so highlie displeased herewith, that he caused his men to arme themselues, and to prepare ladders and other necessarie things to assault the citie: but by the mediation of the French king & curteous excuse of king Tancred (alledging the fault to rest onelie in a sort of rude citizens, whome he promised to punish) the matter was taken vp, and staied for a time, till at length it was perceiued, that the Sicilians subtilie went about to feed king Richard with faire words, till he should be readie to set forwards on his iournie, and so should the matter passe without further punishment.

Herevpon king Richard, not minding to be so mocked at their hands, approched one daie to the wals and gates with his armie in good araie of K. Richard assalteth and entreth the citie by force.battell to giue the assault, which was doone so earnestlie, and so well mainteined, that finallie the citie was entred by force, and manie of the citizens slaine, but the slaughter had béene much greater, if king Richard had not commanded his men to spare the sword, mooued with the lamentable noise of poore people crieng to him for mercie and grace. The Englishmen hauing got possession of the citie pight vp the banners with the armes of the king of England round about the wals, wherewith the French king was sore displeased, and required that the same might be taken downe, and his set vp: but the king of England would not so agrée. Neuerthelesse to pacifie the French kings mood, he deliuered the citie of Messina into the custodie of the knights Templers and Hospitalers, till he might be satisfied of such things as he demanded of king Tancred.

After this on the 8. daie of October, the two kings of England and France, before a great number of earles, barons, and others, both of the The two kings of England and France receiue a solemne oth.cleargie and temporaltie, tooke their solemne othes, that the one should defend the other, and also either others armie in this iournie, both comming and going, without fraud or deceipt: and the like oth was receiued by the earles and barons on both parties. Then the two kings by aduise and consent of both their armies deuised these ordinances.

Ordinances deuised.1 That all pilgrims which chanced to die in this iournie might dispose at their pleasure all their armour, horsses, and apparell, and halfe of those things which they had with them, so that they sent nothing home into their countries, and the other halfe should be at the discretion of Walter archbishop of Rouen, Manser bishop of Langres, of the maister of the temple, and of the maister of the Hospitall, of Hugh duke of Burgoigne, of Rafe de Coucie, of Drogo de Marlow, of Robert Sabuill, Andrew de Chauennie, and [217]of Gilbert Wascoile, which should imploie the same towards the support of the wars in the holie land against the infidels as they thought most expedient.

Plaie forbidden.2 That no man should plaie at anie game within the armie for monie, except knights and chapleins, the which should not loose in one daie and night aboue 20 shillings, they to forfeit an 100 shillings so oft as they lost aboue that summe: the persons aforenamed to haue the same to be distributed as afore is said. The two kings might plaie, and command their seruants in their presence likewise to plaie, so that they excéeded not the summe of 20 shillings. And also the seruants of archbishops, bishops, earles and barons, by their maisters commandement might play, not excéeding that summe: but if anie seruants or mariners, or other of like degrée, were found to play without licence, the seruants should be whipped naked three daies round about the campe, except they ransomed foorth themselues, at the pleasure of the persons aboue named: and the mariners should be plunged ouer head and eares in the sea three mornings togither, after the vse of seamen, except they redeem that punishment, at the discretion likewise of the said persons: and those of other like meane degrées being neither knights nor chapleins should be punished as seruants.

Borrowing.3 That if anie pilgrime borrowed anie thing of an other whilest he was on his iournie, he should be bound to paie it: but if he borrowed it before his setting foorth, he was not bound to answer it till his returne home.

Souldiers or mariners departing from their masters.4 That if anie mariner or seruant, reteined in wages with anie man in this iournie, departed from his master without licence, no other person might receiue him, and if he did, he should be punished at the discretion of the forenamed persons.

Vittelers.5 That no vitteler or other should buy any bread to sell againe, nor any meale within the compasse of the campe, except the same were brought by a stranger, neither might they buy any paast or other thing to sell againe in the campe, or within a league of it.

6 That if anie man bought corne wherof to make bread, it was appointed how much he should gaine in one measure beside the bran.

7 That other occupiers, which vsed buieng and selling of wares, should gaine one penie in 10 pence, neither should anie man refuse anie of the kings coine, except it were broken within the circle.

8 That no man should buy anie flesh to sell it againe, except a liuing beast, which he should kill within the campe.

9 That no man should make bread to sell, but after the rate of penie loaues. Wherin the penie English was appointed to go for foure pence Aniouine. All these ordinances with other were decreed and ordeined to be obserued and kept by the counsell, consent, and agreement of the kings of England, France, and Sicile.

*Polydor.*But to returne now to the dissention betwixt the Englishmen and them of Messina: ye shall vnderstand that the tumult being once ceassed, and diuerse of the chéefe offenders in the late commotion put to death, king Tancred shortlie after came thither, and sought to auoid all suspicion out of king Richards head, that he might conceiue of him for béeing in anie wise culpable in that which his subiects of Messina had attempted against him, and therefore hauing recouered monie of his freends, he restored vnto king Richard the dowrie of his sister quéene Joane, and further offered vnto him to ioine in new alliance with him, offering his daughter in mariage vnto Arthur duke of Britaine, the kings nephue, with a great summe of monie for hir dowrie, if it so should please him.

King Richard accepted the offer, and so ioined in peace and affinitie with the king of Sicile, receiuing of him twentie thousand ounces of gold for the same mariage to be had, and an honorable dowrie assigned foorth of the lands that belonged to the said Arthur for the said ladie to inioy during hir life, in case she suruiued hir husband. And if it so chanced, that by the death of either of them the mariage could not take place, then [218]should king Richard restore the same twentie thousand ounces of gold againe. But beside these twentie thousand ounces of gold thus giuen by king Tancred for the mariage of his daughter, he gaue other twentie thousand ounces to king Richard for an acquitance and quite claime of all manner of duties, rights, and demands, which either he or his sister might pretend, either by reason of anie bequest, dowrie, or anie other manner of waie.

Here is to be noted, that before this conclusion of peace was had, king Richard prouided for his owne defense, in case that king Tancred and his people would haue attempted force against him, in so much that he fortified certeine places, and built a strong castell aloft vpon the top of an hill fast by Messina, which castell he called Mategriffon. Also whereas the admirall of Sicile called Margaret, and one Jordane del Poine, men of great authoritie vnder king Tancred, fled out of Messina with all their families and riches, which they had either in gold or siluer, king Richard seized vpon their houses, their gallies, and possessions, so that he made himselfe as strong as he could, to resist all attempts that might be made against him by his enimies. But now to procéed.

The variance being thus appeased betwixt them, great discord chanced to arise betwixt king Richard and king Philip, who was much offended with king Richard, for that he had thus vsed violence against them of Messina, and compelled king Tancred to agrée with him for monie, to the The lawes of Herberrough.great offense and breach of the lawes of Herberrough, sith the Sicilians verie liberallie aided and furnished the christians armie with vittels and necessarie prouisions. The Frenchmen also had much enuie thereat, Englishmen and Frenchmen fought.that shortlie after vpon a small occasion they picked a quarell against the Englishmen, and from words fell to strokes on both sides, so that there had béene much hurt & slaughter committed, if the two kings had Discord in an armie the hinderer of all profitable enterprises.not doone their best to appease the fraie begun.

But this businesse though it was quietlie as then taken vp and staied, yet bred it such displeasure betwixt the princes and their people, that it turned to the great hurt and hinderance of their good proceedings in their whole enterprise, so that the occasion of a full and perfect victorie easilie slipped out of their hands, as you shall heare hereafter.

An other also of the chéefest causes of grudge betwixt the two kings was, for that king Richard in familiar talke confessed vnto king Philip, that he would marie the king of Nauarres daughter, and cléerelie forsake his sister Adela: which gréeued king Philip not a little, though he dissembled the matter for a time, and rather alledged other causes of displeasure, wherewith to defame king Richard to the world, as one that sought his owne commoditie in spoiling those whom he ought rather to haue defended. But to proceed.

Whilest the English and French armies thus soiourned all the winter time in Sicile, notwithstanding the troubles aforesaid, to the hinderance of king Richards purposes, for the making of his prouisions readie for his iournie, he yet caused engins to be framed, his ships to be newlie calked, rigged and repaired of such hurts as they had receiued both in their long voiage which they had made, and also by certeine wormes, the which during their lieng there, had in diuerse places gnawne and eaten them through to the great danger of their losse, and vtter decaie. Wreckes pardoned.Moreouer at the same time he pardoned all wrecks by sea through all his dominions, releasing for euer all his right to the same, in such wise that euerie person making wrecke by sea, and comming aliue to land, should haue all his goods frée and cleare to himselfe. Furthermore he decréed, that if he chanced to perish in the ship, then his sons and daughters, brethren or sisters, that could prooue themselues to be next heires to him, should haue the same goods; but if he had neither sonne nor daughter, brother nor sister, then should the king haue those goods by waie of his prerogatiue.

This resignation made by king Richard, was confirmed by his charter giuen at Messina in the moneth of October and second yeare of his reigne. Also vpon a godlie [219]repentance wherewith it did please the mercifull God to touch his hart, he called all those prelats togither which were then with him at Messina into the chappell of Reginald de K. Richards confession.Moiac, & there in presence of them all falling downe vpon his knees he confessed the filthie life which he had in lecherous lust before that time led, and humblie receiued penance inioined him by the same bishops, and so became a new man, fearing God, and delighting to liue after his lawes.

Abbat Joachim.Furthermore hearing of the great fame of abbat Joachim, he sent for him ouer into Calabria, who came to Messina, and being asked sundrie questions by king Richard, he made woonderfull answer thereto: as in Houeden and other writers it may appéere, which for breefenesse I passe ouer. About the same time he gaue vnto his nephue Otho, the sonne of his sister Maud, sometime duchesse of Saxonie, the countie of Yorke. But although some were contented to receiue him as their lord, and to doo homage to him, yet other refused him, alledging that they would not renounce their fealties due to the king, till they might sée him againe, & talke with him face to face. Wherevpon the king changing his purpose, gaue vnto the said Otho the countie of Poictou in steed of the said countie of Yorke, as after shall appeere.

1191.The two kings of England and France held their Christmasse this yeare at Messina, and still the king of England vsed great liberalitie in bestowing his treasure freelie amongst knights and other men of warre, The large expenses of K. Richard.so that it was thought he spent more in a moneth than anie of his predecessours euer spent in a whole yeare. In the moneth of Februarie he sent his gallies to Naples, there to receiue his mother and his wife that should be, to wit the ladie Berengaria daughter to the king of Nauarre, and Philip earle of Flanders that came with them. But his mother quéene Elianor and the ladie Berengaria went to Brindize in Puglia, where they were honorablie receiued of Margaret king Tancreds The earle of Flanders.admirall. Moreouer the earle of Flanders comming to Naples, and finding there the gallies of king Richard, went aboord the same, and so came to Messina, at the first following the king of England in all things, till the French king hauing enuie thereat, allured him awaie, and then he hoong altogither on his sléeue. The first daie of March the king of England departed from Messina, to go to the citie of Cathina, there to common with king Tancred, who came thither to meet him.

K. Richard talketh with king Tancred.Here king Richard vnderstood, that the French king had sollicited king Tancred to set vpon the king of England and his armie, to chase them out of his realme: and for the more easie accomplishment thereof, he had promised him his aid, whensoeuer he would giue the aduenture. King Tancred deliuered also to king Richard such letters as the French king had written to him concerning this matter. Wherevpon at his returne to Messina, king Richard shewed by his frowning countenance, that he was nothing pleased with the French king, but sought occasions to get him out of his companie.

The French king perceiuing it, required to vnderstand the cause of this sudden mutation: wherevpon king Richard nothing fearing his power, declared the truth plainelie vnto him by the mouth of the earle of Flanders: and when the other denied the practise, he for proofe of the thing, shewed him the same letters which king Tancred had deliuered vnto him. The French king was not a little abashed hereat, and wist not well what to saie, nor what excuse to make, the matter was so plaine. But yet at length he said: "Well now I perceiue the king of England seeketh to haue some quarell whie he may refuse to marrie with my sister. For these are but forged matters, and no truth resteth in them."

When the king of England vnderstood this maner of answer, he replied in this wise; "That as for the French kings sister, he might not marrie, for as much as he was able to produce good witnesse to prooue that his father had lien with hir and got a child of hir. And as for his priuie procéeding and practise with Tancred, he néeded no further testimonie than his owne hand and his seale, the partie himselfe being present [220]who receiued them, the messenger also being not far off that carried them betwéene both the parties."

When the French king was throughlie informed of the first point, through counsell of the earle of Flanders and others, he pacified himselfe, and was contented to release the king of England of his faith giuen by oth for the contract made with his sister Alice: in consideration of which releasement and deliuerance, the king of England couenanted to giue yearelie to the French king two thousand marks of starling coine for the terme of fiue yeares togither: and at his returne home, it was agreed, that he shuld also deliuer vnto the French king his sister the said ladie Alice, with the towne of Gisors, and all other things which the French king had granted to him with his said sister. On the other part, the French king granted, that the dutchie of Britaine should apperteine to the dominion of the dutchie of Normandie, so as the duke of Britaine should be accompted the liege man of the duke of Normandie, and that the duke of Normandie should answer the French king for both the dutchies, as well of Britaine as Normandie. These agréements were ratified and confirmed with solemne oths receiued, and charters giuen vnder their hands and seales, vpon the 30. of March.

The French king setteth foorth from Messina towards the holie[7] land.About this time the French king (now that the season of the yeare was come) set forward toward the holie land, leauing king Richard behind him in Sicile: and the two and twentith day after his setting foorth from Messina, he arriued at the siege of Acres or Acon. The same day also that the French king departed from Messina, quéene Elianor the mother of king Richard arriued there, bringing with hir the ladie Berengaria the daughter of Sanctius the king of Nauarre, and the fourth day after Quéene Elianor returneth by Rome.quéene Elianor tooke leaue of hir sonne king Richard, and departed homeward towards England, taking hir iournie by Rome about the businesse of Geffrey the elect of Yorke, as to entreat the pope that he would confirme and consecrate him archbishop, or to authorise some other to doo it in his name. The ladie Berengaria remained behind with the kings sister Joane quéene of Sicile.

After this in the moneth of Aprill, on the Wednesday in the passion weeke, king Richard (after he had finished and made an end of all conclusions with king Tancred) did also set forward with his sister Joane, who tooke with hir the ladie Berengaria daughter to the king of Nauarre, affianced to him long before, as aboue is partlie mentioned. *Matth. Paris.* 130. ships and 53. galies saith *Rog. Houed.*His nauie consisted in thirteene mightie great ships with triple sailes, an hundred carikes or rather hulkes, and fiftie gallies. He was no sooner abroad in the maine sea, but a great tempest arose, wherewith his whole nauie was sore tossed and turmoiled vp and downe the seas, and at length driuen on the coast of Cypres, where séeking to take harbour, & to come on land, the Cypriots would not suffer him, but shewed countenance to driue him backe, and to resist his landing. Also whereas six of his ships were so driuen by force of tempest from the residue, that thrée of them perished, and three being cast vpon the shoare of Cypres before the kings arriuall there, the souldiers and other people in the same were compelled to come on land for sauing their liues, where otherwise they stood in danger of drowning, the people of the Ile assailing them in right cruell sort, slue diuerse, and tooke the residue prisoners, and so deteined them for a certeine season.

King Richard then vnderstanding this iniurie to him doone by the Cypriots, & perceiuing they would resist his landing, prepared himselfe and his people to enter vpon them by force. The king of Cypres Isakius or Cursach (whome Houeden nameth emperour of Cypres) had assembled the most part of all the power of men that he might make (though few of them were armed, or had any great skill in feats of warre) and caused them to set boords, logs of wood, benches, formes, and great chests afore them, as a defense, and as it were in steed of a wall, that by succour thereof they might the better kéepe off their enimie from landing.

But K. Richard, so incouraged his men by his presence, & hartened them with such [221]comfortable words as he vttered vnto them, that rowing to the shoare with their galies and small botes, hauing the archers afore them, The Englishmen take land & chase their enimies.they easilie got to land, droue their enimies backe, and so farre pursued them (being but footmen, weatherbeaten, wearie, and weat) as conuenientlie they might, for the shortnes of time. King Richard hauing thus got foot on land, approched the towne of Limezun, which he with his souldiers entred, and finding it emptie of people (which were fled awaie) but full of riches and great plentie of victuals, as corne, wine, oile, and flesh, he seized therevpon.

The same day also the kings sisters and the ladie Berengaria with the residue of the kings nauie entred the hauen of Limezun. In the meane time the king of Cypres (hauing escaped from the battell) got togither his men which were fled and dispersed sundrie waies, and incamped within six miles of king Richard, threatning that the next day he would eftsoones giue battell: which when king Richard vnderstood, he caused his people to be armed the next morning long before day, and so comming by guides vnto the place where the Cypriots with their king were lodged, King Richard with a camisado vanquisheth the Cypriots, & chaseth them out of their campe.*Iohn Textor*.suddenlie they assailed them yer they had anie warning of his marching towards them, by reason whereof they were slaine like beasts in great numbers. Howbeit, their king and a few other escaped and fled away naked, hauing no time to put on their apparell, his treasure, horsse, armour and standard were taken, which standard king Richard straitwaies determined to send vnto saint Edmunds shrine, and so did.

Having thus vanquished his aduersaries, he came backe to Limezun: and the third day after, Guie king of Jerusalem and his brother Geffrey de The K. of Jerusalem and other noble men doo fealtie vnto king Richard.Lucignan with the prince of Antioch Raimond and his sonne named also Raimond earle of Tripoli, with other noble men, arriued at Limezun aforesaid, to visit king Richard, and to offer him their seruices, and so became his men, in swearing fealtie to him against all other persons whatsoeuer.

The same day the king of Cypres perceiuing himselfe vnable to resist the great puissance of king Richards armie, sent ambassadours, and offered to king Richard the summe of twentie thousand marks of gold, in The offers of the king of Cypres.recompense of the monie which his men that were drowned had about them, and also to restore those to libertie which he had taken prisoners, and to make deliuerie to their hands of all their goods. Furthermore he offered to go with him into the holie land personallie, and to serue him with an hundred knights 400 light horssemen, and 500 well armed footmen, The king of Cypres submitteth himselfe.& also to deliuer to king Richard his daughter and heire in hostage, and to acknowledge him his souereigne lord, by swearing to him fealtie for his kingdome, as for that which he should confesse to hold of him.

King Richard accepted these offers, and so the king of Cypres came in and sware fealtie to king Richard, in presence of the king of Jerusalem, the prince of Antioch, and other barons, and promised vpon his oth then receiued, not to depart till all things couenanted on his part were performed. Then king Richard assigned tents for him and his to lodge in, and appointed certeine knights and other men of warre to haue the custodie of him. But the same day after dinner vpon repentance of that which he had doone, he deceiued his keepers and stale awaie, sending knowledge backe to the king that he would not stand to the couenants, which were concluded vpon betwixt them.

King Richard seemed to like the matter well enough, and foorthwith deliuered a part of his armie vnto the king of Jerusalem and to the prince of Antioch, appointing them to persue the king of Cypres by land, whilest he with one part of his gallies and Robert de Turneham with the other might search about the coast by sea, to prohibit his passage by water. In euerie place where they came, such ships and gallies as they found they seized into their hands, and no resistance was made against them, by reason the people fled to the woods and mountains, leauing the cities, townes and castels void in all stéeds, where the king or the Robert de Turneham.said sir Robert de Turneham with their vessels began to appéere. [222]When they had taken their pleasure thus alongst the coasts, they returned againe vnto Limezun. The king of Jerusalem and the other that went foorth by land, when they could not spéed of their purpose, returned also, in which meane time a great number of Cypriots came in, and submitting themselues to king Richard, were receiued as his subiects.

On the 12. daie of Maie, the ladie Berengaria daughter to the king of The king of England marieth the ladie Berengaria. She is crowned quéene.Nauarre was maried according to a precontract vnto king Richard at Limezun aforesaid in the Ile of Cypres, one of the kings chaplins executing the order of the marriage. The same daie also she was crowned by the bishop of Eureux, the archbishops of Apamea and Aux, with the bishop of Baion ministring vnto him. After the solemnitie of this marriage and coronation ended, king Richard set forward with his armie into the countrie of Cypres, and first wan (by surrender) the citie of Nichosia, and after the strong castell of Cherin, within the which was the daughter of the king of Cypres, which ladie humblie yeelded hir selfe vnto K. Richard, (who counting it reproach to be extreme with such as submit themselues, and speciallie the female sex, according to the old saieng,

Pacere subiectis nobilis scit ira leonis)

had pitie of hir case, and sent hir to his wife the new quéene, willing that she might be honorablie vsed. From thence passing forward, these Castels deliuered to the king of England.castels were deliuered into his hands, Baffes and Buffeuent, Den, Amur, Candace, and afterwards all the other castels and cities, townes and places of strength within that Ile one after an other. Finallie, hearing The king of Cyprus again submitteth himselfe to the king of England.that the king of Cypres was inclosed in an abbie called Cap S. Andrew, he marched thitherwards: but when the king of Cypres heard of his approch, he came foorth and submitted himselfe wholie into his hands. The king first appointed him to the kéeping of his chamberlaine Rafe Rafe Fitz Geffrey.Fitz Geffrey, and after sent him into the citie of Tripoli, there to be kept in close prison. Who when he heard he should be committed to close prison, and remaine in fetters, said, "that if he laie in irons, he should shortlie end his life." Wherevnto king Richard when he heard of it, answered: "He saith well, and therefore bicause he is a noble man, and our mind is not to haue him dead, but onelie to be kept safe from starting anie more awaie, and dooing new hurt, let him be chained in giues and fetters made of siluer," and so he was.

But to procéed. After the king had set the countrie of Cypres in good staie, he deliuered the keeping thereof vnto Richard de Camuille and He arriued there on the saturdaie in Whitsunwéek, being the saturdaie also next before the feast of S. Barnabie. *Galfridus.Vinsant.*Robert de Turneham. This doone vpon the wednesdaie in the Whitsunwéeke he tooke the sea againe, and passed ouer to the citie of Acres, which as then was besieged by the christian armie, as ye may read in the description of the holie land, onelie giuing you to vnderstand, that such was the valiancie of king Richard shewed in manfull constreining of the citie, that his praise was greatlie bruted both amongst the christians and also the Saracens.

Howbeit the secret enimitie betwixt him and the French king eftsoones reuiued, by occasion of such discord as chanced betwixt Guido king of Jerusalem, and Conrade the marques of Tire, so that parties were taken, and whereas both the Pisans and Geneuois did offer their seruice vnto king Richard, yet bicause the Geneuois were confederat with the French king, who tooke part with the marques, he refused them, and receiued the Pisans and Geneuois.Pisans, ioining himselfe with king Guido to support him against his enimies.

Here is to be remembred, that before king Richard arriued at the siege, he incountred on the sea a mightie great ship called a Drommond, which *Matt. Paris. Nic. Triuet.*Saphaldine the brother of Saladine.one Saphaldine the brother of Saladine a prince of the Saracens had sent, to refresh them with vittels. This ship king Richard caused féercelie to be assailed with his gallies, and at length bowged hir with all the vittels and prouision within the same, as wild-fire, barels of firie serpents, armour and weapons of sundrie sorts, besides all the mariners and men of warre, except such as were taken to mercie and saued aliue, being about 200 in the whole, whereas there were aboord the same *Matth. Paris. N. Triuet.*ship 500 men of warre, as some write, though other haue but 800.

[223]¶ But now to other accidents that chanced this yere. On Midsummer eeue there was such an eclipse of the sunne, the moone being the same time 27 *An eclipse of the sunne.*daies old, that for the space of thrée houres (for so long it lasted) such darkness came ouer the face of the earth, that euen in the daie *The seuenth houre of the daie saith Matth. Paris.*time (for this eclipse began about nine of the clocke in the morning) the stars appeared plainelie in the element.

In the same moneth of June, Richard de Camuille, whome the king had left (as ye haue heard) gouernour in Cypres, chanced to fall sicke, and *Richard de Camuille deceasseth.*comming without licence to the siege of Acres, there died. After whose death the Cypriots and those called Griffones and Ermians reuolted from the English obedience, and chose to them a king, one that was a moonke of the familie of Isachus their former king: but Robert de Turneham, who after the deceasse of Richard Camuille remained sole gouernour of the Ile, gathered a power of men togither, and giuing battell to the new king (whom Houeden nameth also emperour) vanquished him with his complices, tooke him prisoner, and hanged him on a paire of galowes. The same moneth also died Rafe Fitz Geffrey, who had the other king Isac in custodie, and then king Richard deliuered him to the knights of the hospitall, who sent him to the castell of Margant, there safelie to be kept as prisoner to the vse of the king of England.

Now will we returne vnto the affaires of England and make some mention of the dooings there. Yee shall vnderstand, that after king Richard was set forward on his iournie, William Longchampe lord chancellour and *Polydor.*bishop of Elie, appointed (as ye haue heard) gouernour of the realme, began to exercise his authoritie to the vttermost, taking vpon him the state of a prince, rather than of a subiect. He had of late (as before ye haue heard) procured such fauor at the hands of pope Clement, that he *The Lord chancellor called the popes legat in England.*was instituted by him legat of the apostolike see here in England, so that pretending a rule both ouer the clergie and temporaltie, and by reason that he had both the authoritie of pope and king in his hands, he vsed the same to his most aduantage, as well in causes ecclesiasticall as temporall, whereby he wrought manie oppressions both against them of *The statelie port of the lord chancellor. Ran. Higd.*the clergie and temporaltie. He mainteined such a port and countenance in his dooings, that he would ride with a thousand horsses, by meanes whereof when he came to lie at abbeis and other places (bringing with him such a traine) he was verie burdenous vnto them, speciallie when he laie at their houses any space of time.

A conuocation.This man called a conuocation at Westminster, wherein at the suit of Hugh Nouant bishop of Chester, it was decreed, that the moonks of *Moonks of Couentrie displaced. Polydor.Ran. Higd. Wil. Paruus.*The occasion. *Ran. Higd.*Couentrie should be displaced, and secular canons brought into that house to supplie their roomes. Which was doone by the authoritie of the said lord chancellour, being bribed by the foresaid bishop of Chester (as some writers haue recorded) for displeasure which he bare to the moonks, by reason of a fraie which they had made vpon the said bishop in their church at Couentrie, and drawne bloud of him before the alter there, as he alledged.

*Wil. Paruus.*But some haue written, that the bishop of Chester procured a licence of the pope, to alter the state of that church in sort aboue mentioned, which is most likelie, surmising against the moonks, that they were most manifest and stubborne disturbers of that peace and quietnesse which ought to remaine amongst churchmen: and yet he himselfe sowed the strife *Ran. Higd. Polydor.*and dissention amongst them, and namelie betwéene the prior and his couent. Moreouer, the said lord chancellour depriued such rulers of their administrations and gouernements, as the king had appointed to beare any high authoritie within the realme, pretending not onelie the kings commandement, but also alleadging a reason which mooued him so to doo, as thus, that he might thereby take awaie all occasions of grudges from the people, which otherwise might thinke, and would not sticke to *The L.*

chancellors reason.
The bishop of Durham.
The bishop of Winchester.saie, that they were oppressed by the rule of manie kings in stéed of one king. He did also depriue Hugh the bishop of Durham of all his honour and dignitie, and put the bishop of Winchester to great trouble. Moreouer, doubting least the Nobles of the realme would rise against him, and put him out of his place; he sought to kéepe them lowe, and spoiled [224]them of their monie and substance. Likewise pretending a colour The lord chancellors meaning to kéepe earle John lowe.of doubt, least earle John the kings brother should attempt any thing against his brother the king now in his absence, he sought also to kéepe him vnder. To be bréefe, he plaied in all points the right part of a tyrant, and shewed himselfe such a one in all respects as mainteined his title,

*Pal. in suo cap.*Non disceptando aut subtilibus argumentisVincere, sed ferro mauult sua iura tueri,Pontifices nunc bella iuuant, sunt cætera nuga,Nec præcepta patrum nec Christi dogmata curant,Iactant se dominos rerum & sibi cuncta licere.

At length the king receiued aduertisement from his mother queene Elianor of his demeanor, and that there was great likeliehood of some commotion to insue, if spéedie remedie were not in time prouided. Wherevpon being Walter the archbishop of Rouen sent into England.then in Sicile, he sent Walter the archbishop of Rouen into England with commission, to ioine in administration of the kingdome with his chancellor of the said bishop of Elie. But the archbishop comming into England was so slenderlie interteined of the chancellour, and in effect so litle regarded, that notwithstanding his commission and instructions He is little regarded of the lord chancellor.brought from the king, he could not be permitted to beare any rule. But the chancellour deteining the same wholie in his hands, ordered all things at his pleasure, without making the archbish. of Rouen, or any other of counsel with him, except such as it pleased him to admit for the seruing of his owne turne.

¶ He certeinelie beléeued (as manie other did) that king Richard would neuer returne with life into England againe, which caused him to attempt so manie vnlawfull enterprises, and therefore he got into his hands all the castels and fortresses belonging to the crowne, and furnished them with garisons of souldiers, as he thought necessarie, depriuing such capteins of their roomes as he suspected not to fauour his procéedings.

One Gerard de Camuille had bought of the king the kéeping of the castell of Lincolne, vnto whome also the sheriffewike of the shire was committed for a time, but the lord chancellour, perceiuing that he bare more good will vnto earle John the kings brother than to him (which John he most suspected) he tooke from him the shiriffewike, & demanded also to haue the castell of Lincolne deliuered into his hands, which Gerard refused to deliuer, and perceiuing that the chancellor would practise to haue it by force, he fled vnto earle John, requiring him of competent aid and succour.

The chancellor on the other part, perceiuing what hatred diuerse of the Nobles bare him, thought good to prouide for his owne suertie the best that he could, and therefore sent for a power of men from beyond the sea: but bicause he thought it too long to staie till they arriued, he The lord chancellor besiegeth the castell of Lincolne. Earle John winneth the castels of Notingham and Tickhill.came to Lincolne with such power as he could make, and besieged the castell. Erle John the kings brother aduertised hereof, raised such numbers of men as he might make of his freends, seruants and tenants, and with small a doo wan the castels of Notingham and Tickhill within two daies space. This doone, he sent to the lord chancellour, commanding him either to breake vp his siege, or else to prepare for battell. The chancellour considering with himselfe that there was small trust to be put in diuerse of those lords that were with him, bearing good will to The chancellor raiseth his siege with dishonour.earle John, and but hollow harts towards him, raised his siege and departed with dishonour.

Not long after, one of his hornes was broken off by the death of pope Clement, whereby his power legantine ceased: wherewith being somewhat The lord chancellor and earle John are agréed. The chancellor breaketh the agréement.abashed, he came to a communication with earle John, and vpon certeine conditions made peace with him. Shortlie after the souldiers which he had sent for, arriued in England, and then he began to go from the agréement made with

21

earle John, affirming that he would either driue the same earle out of England, or else should earle John doo the like to him: for it was not of sufficient largenesse to hold them both. Howbeit, shortlie after, a peace was eftsoones concluded betwixt them with The lord chancellor and earle John make another agréement.condition, that if it chanced king Richard to depart [225]this life before his returne into England, not leauing any issue of his bodie begotten, that then the chancellour renouncing the ordinance made by king Richard (who had instituted his nephue Arthur duke of Britaine to be his heire and successour) should consent to admit earle John for king of England, contrarie to the said ordinance.

But in the meane time it was agréed, that earle John should deliuer vp the castels of Notingham and Tickhill, Notingham to the hands of William Marshall, and Tickhill to the hands of William Wendenall, they to kéepe the same vnto the vse and behoofe of king Richard, that vpon his returne he might doo with them as should please him: prouided that if it so chanced, that he should die before he could returne from his voiage, or that the chancellour went from the agréement now taken, then immediatlie should the foresaid castels of Notingham and Tickhill be restored vnto earle John.

Moreouer, the other castels of such honours as were assigned to earle John by the king his brother, were committed vnto the custodie of certeine persons of great trust and loialtie, as the castell of Wallingford to the archbishop of Rouen, the castell of Bristow to the bishop of Lincolne, the castell of the Peake to the bishop of Couentrie, the castell of Bolesofres vnto Richard de Peake (or if he refused, then should the bishop of Couentrie haue it in kéeping) the castell Eie was committed to Walter Fitz Robert, the castell of Herford to Roger Bigot, and to Richard Reuell the castell of Excester and Launston. These persons to whom these castels were thus committed to be kept, receiued also an oth, that they should faithfullie kéepe them to the kings behoofe, and if he chanced to die, before he should returne, then the same should be deliuered vnto earle Johns hands. Also there were three Castels deliuered in trust to the keeping of certeine persons.castels that perteined to the crowne, deliuered likewise in trust, as the castell of Windsor vnto the earle of Arundell, the castell of Winchester vnto Gilbert de Lacie, and the castell of Northampton vnto Simon de Pateshull.

It was also agréed, that bishops, abbats, earles, and barons, valuasors, and freeholders should not be disseised of their lands, goods or chattels, otherwise than by order of the iustices or officers of the king, so that they should be iudged in the kings courts according to the lawfull customes and ordinances of the realme, and likewise that earle John should cause the same orders to be obserued through all his lands. Prouided that if any man attempted to doo otherwise vpon support or maintenance of earle John, he should stand to be reformed by the archbishop of Rouen if he chanced then to be in England, and by the kings iustices, and by those that had sworne to obserue this peace: and also earle John himselfe at their request should see such reformation to be had.

Moreouer, it was agréed that all those castels that had bin built or begun to be builded since the kings passage ouer towards his iournie, should be razed, and no new made or fortified till his returne, except in manours perteining to the kings demaine, if need required, or by his speciall commandement, either by letters, or sufficient messengerrs. That the shiriffewike of Lincolne, which the lord chancellour had assigned vnto William de Stuteuille should be restored to Gerard de Camuille, who had a daie appointed him to appéere in the kings court, to heare what might be laid against him: and if such matter could be prooued, for the which he ought to loose the said shiriffewike and the castell of Lincolne, then he should depart from them by the iudgement of the court, or else not. Neither should earle John mainteine him against the iudgement of that court, nor should receiue any outlawes, or such as were notoriouslie knowen for enimies to the king, and so named, nor should suffer them to be receiued within the precinct of his liberties.

To hold, mainteine and obserue this peace, the said earle and chancellour sware in the hand of the archbishop of Rouen with seuen barons on either part. On the part of earle John these were the names of them that receiued the oth: Stephan Ridell his chancellour, William de la Mare, Robert de la Mare, Philip de Turechester, William de Kahennes, Gilbert Basset & William de Montacute. On the chancellours part, the earles of Arundell and Salisburie, earle Roger Bigot, and the earle of Clare, with Walter Fitz [226]Robert, William de Breuse, and

22

Roger Fitz Ramfrey. These things were concluded in this sort, the authoritie and commandement of the king yet in all things saued and reserued: but so, that if before his returne he should signifie his pleasure to the contrarie of the ordinances aboue mentioned, then should the castels of Notingham and Tickhill be restored vnto earle John, notwithstanding what An. Reg. 3.soeuer the king should command touching the same. Thus was the peace *Matth. West. Polydor.*concluded eftsoones betwixt earle John and the chancellour.

Geffrey the archbishop of Yorke. *Rog. Houed.*In this meane while, Geffrey the elect archbishop of Yorke, after long suit and manie delaies contriued, speciallie by the chancellour, obteined his pall, being consecrated by the archbishop of Towrs, by virtue of his buls obteined from pope Celestine. The chancellour aduertised herof, and vnderstanding that he meant to come shortlie into England to be installed, was in a great chafe, bicause that during the time of the vacation, he had vsed the reuenues of that see at his pleasure, and therefore now to forego them he was nothing contented. *Matth. Paris.*Herevpon he wrote his letters vnto Matthew de Clare shiriffe of Kent in this forme.

The lord chancellours letters to the shiriffe of Kent.

Præcipimus tibi quòd si Eboracen. Electus ad aliquem portum in balliua tua applicuerit, aut aliquis nunciorum eius, eum retineri facias, donec mandatum nostrum indè receperis. Et similiter præcipimus, quòd omnes literas papæ aut magni alicuius viri quæ illic venerint, facias retineri. The English whereof is thus.

"We command you that if the elect of Yorke shall arriue at any port or hauen within your bailiwicke, or any messenger of his, that you cause them to be arested and kept, till you haue commandement from vs therein. And we command you likewise, to stay, attach, and keepe all letters that come from the pope, or any other great man."

Polydor. The death of the archbishop of Canturbury.*Io. Textor.*Likewise, whereas Baldwine archbishop of Canturburie, hauing taken his iournie into the holie land, and arriuing there before the king, chanced to depart this life at Tyrus, the last yeere, vpon the feast daie of S. Edmund, the chancellour found meanes to keepe that sée also vacant, that he might receiue the profits thereof, during the vacation, and find meanes to be prepared to it in the end. But as touching the sée of Yorke, although he had (as before is said) made his hand of the reuenues belonging to the same from time to time at his pleasure, yet now after that he heard how Geffrey had receiued the pall, he made hauocke, wasting & spoiling all that would yeeld him anie monie, without respect of right or wrong. Moreouer, he caused the hauens to be watched, with commandement giuen to the townes on the sea coast, that they should not The archbishop arriued and is committed to ward.suffer the archbishop Geffrey to take land. At length yet he arriued at Douer, where he was by the aforesaid Matthew de Clare first staied, and after taken out of the abbeie by the chancellours commandement, and committed to prison within the castell, where a Noble man that had maried the chancellors sister was capteine.

The newes of whose imprisonment was anon bruted through the realme, wherewith the Nobles fretted, and the commons curssed: finallie all men detested such tyrannie in the chancellour. But namelie the kings brother earle John stormed at the matter, and with all spéed assembled an armie out of those places where he bare rule, increasing the number with a power of Welshmen. There came to him the bishop of Winchester, with manie earles and barons, also the bishop of Bath and Chester, which latelie before had béene chéefe fauourers of the chancellour in all his dooings: but now that the world was [227]changed, they shewed themselues the most earnest enimies he had, as well in words as déeds.

In an assemblie of all the bishops of England, all those were excommunicate in solemne wise, with candels light, and other such ceremonies, which had either giuen commandement, or were present as partakers, to pull out of the church the archbishop of Yorke, or his people by violence, and had imprisoned them in maner (as before yée haue heard:) but this was after the archbishop was set at libertie, as shuld appeare by Matthew Paris, for the chancellour repenting himselfe (though now too late) of his cruell dealing against the archbishop of Yorke, wherewith he had kindled such a brand against him, commanded the said archbishop (namelie at the instant sute of the bishop of London, or rather at the commandement of earle John, as Houeden saith) to be set at libertie. But the displeasure once kindled in the hearts of the Nobles, could not so easilie[8] be quenched with his deliuerie, as it was spéedilie set on fire by his imprisonment, so that they being now in armour, purposed to abate the pride of the chancellour, and to deliuer the R. *Houed.* The chancellour summoned to appeare.common-wealth, of such an vglie tyrant. And to begin, they summoned, and assigned him a peremptorie day to appeare at Reading, to make answer vnto such iniuaries as he had doone against the archbishop of Yorke, and the bishop of Durham, sithens the departure of his souereigne lord the king.

At which day there came to Reading earle John, and the archbishop of Rouen, with manie other bishops, earles, and barons, abiding there all that day, to sée if the chancellour would appeare or no; but he came not: wherevpon they prepared to march foorth towards London, and therewithall set forward in like maner. He on the other side being a man of a great courage, had gathered an armie of such strangers and other his fréends as he could make, and therewith went foorth, and encamped néere to Windsor, there to abide his aduersaries, and to giue them battell, if they came forward and would abide it. But when they approched, and he perceiued also how diuerse of his freends shranke from him, and went to his enimies, he durst not attempt the hazard of a The chauncellour retireth to London.field, but fled backe to London, and there withdrew into the tower, with all his host, bicause he durst not commit himselfe to the doubtfull fellowship of the citizens. Through his great pride and statelie port which he mainteined, as partlie yée haue heard, he had procured to himselfe no small hatred amongst all degrees of men, and namelie such as by the kings appointment ought to haue béene parteners with him in gouernement of the realme sore repined at his presumptuous proceedings, for that he disdained (as it séemed) to vse their aduise, or to ioine them with him in the administration of things, so that now in time of his trouble he wist not in whome he might put his trust.

After he was thus retired into the tower of London, earle John, the archbishop of Rouen, and the other bishops, earles, and barons associated togither against him, followed him at the héeles, entered the citie, and besieged the tower on ech side. On the morrow after, being the fourth day after the octaues of saint Michaell, they came togither into Paules church-yard, where they publikelie declared the iniurious A declaration made against the lord chancellour.wrongs doone and practised by the chancellour; namelie against the archbishop of Yorke, and the bishop of Durham. Those also that had béene appointed as associats with him, accused him, in that he had taken vpon him to rule and gouerne all things after his owne will, not vouchsafing to haue their aduise or councell in such sort as had béene conuenient.

The archbishop of Rouen and William Marshall earle of Pembroke shewed there before all the people the kings letters which he had sent from The tenor of this letter shall héereafter appeare.Messina, appointing that they should be associats with him in gouernment of the kingdome; and that without the counsell and aduice of them and others assigned thereto, he should not meddle with the rule of the land, and that if he should doo any thing to the hinderance of the common-wealth, or sécke to meddle with the affaires of the realme, without their good aduise, that then he should be deposed. Héerevpon it seemed good to earle John, and to all the bishops, earles and barons of the realme, and to the citizens of London, there assembled, that the [228]said chancellour should be deposed, and so they proceeded, and deposed him in déed, appointing the archbishop of Rouen in his place, who would not take vpon him to doo anie thing touching the rule of the land, without consent of his associats assigned to him, and the barons or the eschecker.

The same day, earle John, and the archbishop of Rouen, and other of the The citizens of London.kings iustices, granted to the citizens of London the priuilege of their communaltie; and the said earle and archbishop, and in maner all the bishops, erls and barons of the realme sware to mainteine the said priuilege firme and stable, so long as should please their souereigne lord. And the citizens of London sware to be true, and to doo their faithfull seruice vnto king Richard and his heirs, and if he chanced to die without issue, then to receiue earle John the brother of king Richard for their king and souereigne lord, and therevpon sware fealtie to him against all men, sauing that which they owed vnto his brother king Richard.

The chancellour perceiuing the multitude to be such which he had with him in the tower, as the place was not able to hold them any long time, The chancellour yéeldeth vp the tower.after he had remained within it one night, he came foorth vnto earle John, and to the other that were thus entred the citie, and now readie to besiege him, of whome he got licence for them that were inclosed within the tower, to depart without damage, and therewith deliuered vp the tower into the hands of the archbishop of Rouen, with the castell of Windsor, and certeine other castels, which he held within the realme, but not all: notwithstanding he couenanted to make deliuerie of the residue, which yet remained in the hands of them whome he had appointed to the kéeping of the same. And for assurance of that couenant to be performed before he departed the realme, he deliuered his brethren, and one that was his chamberleine, to remaine with the lords as hostages.

This doone, he hasted to Canturburie, where he promised to receiue the crosse of a pilgrime to go into the holie land, and to render vp the crosse of his legatship, which he had vsurped a yeare and a halfe after the death of pope Clement, to the preiudice of the church of Rome, and to the detriment and great hinderance of the English church. For there was not any church within the realme, which had not béene put to fine The print of the legats crosse.and ransome by that crosse, nor any ecclesiasticall person went frée, but the print of the crosse appeared in him and his purse. From Canturburie he got him to Douer to his brother in law, and finallie séeking means to passe ouer into France, and doubting to be discouered, he apparelled himselfe in womans raiment, & got a web of cloth on his The bishop of Elie late lord chancellor disguiseth himselfe in womans apparell. He is bewraied.arme, as though he had béene some housewifelie woman of the countrie: but by the vntowardlie folding and vncunning handling of his cloth (or rather by a lewd fisherman that tooke him for an harlot) he was suspected and searched so narrowlie, that by his priuie members he was prooued to be a man, and at length knowne, attached, and committed to prison, after he had béene reprochfullie handled by them that found him, and by the wiues of the towne, in such vnséemlie apparell.

Earle John would haue had him punished, and put to some open reproofe for his passed tyrannicall dooings; but the bishops, and other of the Earle John not ye bishops fréend.barons, for reuerence of his order, procured his deliuerance, with licence to passe ouer into Normandie where he was borne. Thus was the bishop of Elie a man full of pride and couetousnesse ouerthrowne with shame, and receiued for his hie climing a reprochfull downefall: for none are more subiect to ruine and rebuke, than such as be aloft and supereminent ouer others, as the poet noteth well saieng:

*Ouid. lib. 1. de. rem. am.*Summa petit liuor, perflant altissima venti,Summa petunt dextra fulmina missa Iouis.

*Matth. Paris.*In time he was deposed from his office of being chancellour, and not without warrant, for in verie déed, king Richard hauing receiued aduertisements from the lords and péeres of the realme, of the chancellours presumptuous and hautie demeanour, with wrongs offered to diuerse persons, wrote to them againe as followeth.
[229]

A letter of king Richard directed to the States of the land for the deposing of the bishop of Elie from his office of lord chancellour.

Richard king of England sendeth greeting to William Marshall, to Gilbert Fitz Peter, and Henrie Berdulfe, and to William Brewer, péeres. If it so chance that our chancellour hath not faithfullie handled the affaires and businesse of our realme (committed vnto him) by the aduise and counsell of you, and others to whome we haue also assigned the charge of gouernement of the same realme: we command you, that according to your disposition in all things to be doone concerning the gouernement thereof, you order and dispose as well for eschetes, as all other things, &c.

By force of this commission, the lords were the bolder to procéed against him as ye haue heard. Now after his comming into the parties The bishop of Elie complaineth of his wrongs receiued.beyond the seas, he ceassed not with letters and messengers to present his complaint to the pope of Rome, and to king Richard of the iniuries receiued at the hands of earle John and his complices. Herevpon pope Celestine wrote in déed to all the archbishops and bishops that were The popes letters vnto the archbishope and bishops of

England. within the realme of England, in behalfe of the said bishop of Elie, declaring, that for so much as the king of England was gone into the holie land to warre against the enimies of our faith, leauing his kingdome vnder the protection of the apostolike see, he could not but haue speciall regard to see that the state, rights and honour thereof were preserued from all danger of decaie.

Note how the pope defendeth his chaplins. Wherefore, vnderstanding that there had beene certeine attempts made by John erle of Mortaigne and others, both against the king and the bishop of Elie, that was not onelie legat of the apostolike sée, but also gouernour of the land appointed by the king, which attempt sounded greatlie to the reproch of the church of Rome, and danger of damage to insue to king Richard, if remedie were not the sooner found: therefore he commanded them by the vertue of their obedience, to excōmunicat the earle of Mortaigne, or any other that was knowne to haue laid any violent hands vpon the said bishop of Elie, or deteined him as captiue, or inforced him to any oth, or else had changed the state of rule in the kingdome of England to other forme, than king Richard had ordeined at his setting forward towards the holie land: and that not onelie all the councellours, authors, aiders and complices of those that had committed such outrage, but also their lands should stand interdicted, so that no diuine seruice should be vsed within the precinct of the same, except penance and christning of infants. This to remaine till the said bishop & kingdome were restored into the former estate: and that the parties excommunicated should present themselues with letters from the bishops vnto the apostolike see to be absolued, etc.

Herevpon also the bishop of Elie himselfe wrote vnto the bishop of Lincolne and other, touching this matter: but the bishops did neither any thing in accomplishment of the effect of the popes letters, nor at his owne supplication. And therefore perceiuing small helpe to come that waie, he sought to obteine the fauour and fréendship of earle John, and of his mother quéene Elianor. In the meane time, the lords, barons and prelates of the realme, after they had depriued him of all authoritie, and banished him out of the land, ordeined the archbishop of Rouen in The archbishop of Rouen chéefe gouernour of England. fauour of the kings commission, to haue the chéefe rule and administration of things touching all the affaires of the common-wealth; but yet so as earle John had the dooings in manie points, so that he might séeme in manner an associat with him, whereof sprang much inconuenience. For this [230]John being a man (as he is noted by some writers) of an ambitious nature, was suspected to aspire vnto the kingdome: in somuch that he had ioined with the French king, after the same king was returned foorth of the holie land, against his brother king Richard, if his mother quéene Elianor had not persuaded him to the contrarie.

R. Houed. Wil. Paruus. Fiftene saith *Functius*, but others agrée with *Houed.* as*Gerardus Mercator* citing*Albericus* a moonke. Whilest these things were a dooing, on the twelfth daie of Julie, the citie of Acres was surrendred into the Christian mens hands, for the Soldan Saladine (being approched néere to the siege of the christians with a puissant armie, in hope to haue raised their siege) when he perceiued it laie not in his power to worke any feat to the succour of his people within the citie, and that they were so constreined that they must néeds yéeld, he holpe to make their composition, and promised to performe certeine couenants on their behalfe. Herevpon, the Saracens within Acres couenanted not onelie to deliuer the citie vnto the christians with fiue hundred prisoners of christians which they had within the same, but also to procure that the holie crosse should be to them deliuered, with a thousand other christian prisoners, such as the christian princes should appoint out of those numbers which Saladine had in his custodie, and further, to giue them two hundred thousand Besans. And till these couenants were performed, it was agréed, that the Saracens, which were at that present left within the citie, should remaine as pledges, vnder condition, that if the same couenants were not performed within fortie daies, then should they stand at the mercie of the christian princes as touching life and lim.

The citie of Acres. These things thus concluded, and the citie yéelded vp into the christian mens hands, the French king vpon enuie and malice conceiued against king Richard (although he pretended sicknesse for excuse) departed homewards, The French K. returneth home.setting from Acres the last day of Julie. Now then, after the departure of king Philip, when the day approched, in the which the Saracens should performe the couenants; or else stand to the iudgement of life and death at the pleasure of the christian princes: it was perceiued that the couenants would not be fulfilled according to the agréement. For Saladine, as it well appeared, ment not to performe that which for the safegard of his men he had vndertaken, and did but dallie with the christians to prolong the time: wherevpon sentence was giuen foorth, that for default in such behalfe, the Saracens remaining as pledges should loose their heads.

Saladine hauing knowledge thereof, sent word to king Richard and to the whole christian armie, that if his people that were in the christian mens hands lost their heads, he would not faile but cause the heads of all those christians which he had in captiuitie to be cut off also. Notwithstanding which answer, on the fourteenth day of August king Richard issued foorth of the citie, passing the vttermost ditches, and incamped himselfe neere the armie of Saladine, who the same daie sent rich presents vnto king Richard, requiring of him a longer day for performance of the couenants, but that would not be granted. Wherefore Saladine causeth the christian prisoners to be beheaded.vpon the said deniall, Saladine caused all those christian prisoners which he had in his hands to be beheaded on the eightéenth day of August, on which day king Richard aduanced foorth towards the lodgings of the Saracens, and skirmished with them verie hotlie, so that manie were wounded and slaine on both parts: and amongst other one of king Richards companions at all exercises named Peter Mignot lost his life there. Furthermore, although king Richard knew that Saladine had put the christian prisoners to death in such wise as you haue heard, yet would not he preuent his terme appointed for the execution of the Saracens that were in his custodie, but abiding vnto the twentith day of August, he then caused those Saracens which fell to his lot, at the time of the surrender of Acres, being in number about 2600. to be brought foorth of the citie, and néere to the walles in the sight of Saladine and all his host they had their heads chopped off. The duke of Burgoigne caused execution to be doone within the citie vpon those which fell to the French kings share, the number of the which rose to two thousand and foure hundred, or thereabouts: for the whole number was reckoned to be about fiue thousand that thus lost their liues through the inconstancie of their prince: yet diuerse of [231]the principall had their liues saued. The Saracens themselues also spake much euill of Saladine for this R. Houed.matter, bicause that refusing to performe the articles of couenants, he had occasioned the enimie to slea those that had so valiantlie serued in defense of the citie, to the vttermost ieopardie of their liues. And heere is verified that knowne verse,

Quicquid delirant reges plectuntur Achiui.

*Ger. Dor.*But now to leaue forren matters, and to returne home into England: we find, that on the second of December, the monks of Canturburie chose to their archbishop Reignold bishop of Bath, who within fifteene daies after his election, departed this life, and lieth buried at Bath. Also this yeare, or (as Ger. Dor. saith) in the yeare following, the bishop Strife betwixt ye archbishop of York and the bishop of Durham.of Durham sought meanes to withdraw his subiection from the archbishop of Yorke, for which attempt the archbishop of Yorke, vpon trust of the popes grant, did not excommunicate the said bishop, notwithstanding that he appealed to the popes consistorie three seuerall times, putting his owne matter and his churches to be examined and tried by the pope, where vpon he obeied not the excommunication: and signifieng the cause vnto Rome, obtained such fauour, that the pope and his cardinals reuersed the sentence, and iudged the excommunication to be of none effect. And further they decreed, that if the archbishop of Yorke had broken the altars and chalices, as information was giuen, in which the bishop of Durham had celebrated after his appeale made to the court of Rome, that then should the said bishop of Durham be acquited from owing any subiection to the said archbishop for so long as they two should liue togither.

True it is, that the archbishop had not onelie broken the altars and chalices which the bishop had vsed in déed for the celebration of masse, but also held his owne brother John earle of Mortaigne for excommunicate, bicause he had eat and dronke in companie of the said bishop, and would not communicate with him, till he came to receiue absolution, and to make satisfaction for his fault. In the end the bishops of Lincolne and Rochester, with the abbat of Peterburrow, were appointed by the pope to haue the hearing of this matter, as iudges authorised by his buls, who sat therevpon at Northampton, vpon S. Calixt his day, where after they had heard both parties argue what they could in either of their cases, they gaue a longer day, to wit, vntill the feast of the natiuitie of saint John Baptist next after, to see if by anie good means there might some agréement haue béene had betwixt them, or (if that could not be) that then the popes leters should stand in force as before, & the helpes of either part saued, as though no delaie had béene vsed. And to this, both parties were agréeable, speciallie at the motion of the bishop of Lincolne.

Roger Lacie conestable of Chester.This yeare also, Roger de Lacie conestable of Chester tooke Alan de Lec and Peter de Bouencort, and vpon despite hanged them, for that being put in trust amongst other with the kéeping of the castels of Notingham and Tickhill, which he had receiued into his custodie of the bishop of Elie quondam lord chancellour, they had consented to the treason of Robert de Crokeston, & Eudo de Duuille, which deliuered the same castels vnto John earle of Mortaigne. The same earle of Mortaigne was highlie offended for the death of those two persons, and therefore wasted the lands of the said Roger which lay within the compasse of his iurisdiction.

But now touching the departure of the French king from Acres, diuerse occasions are remembred by writers of the emulation and secret spite which he should beare towards king Richard, and beside other alreadie touched, one was for enterteining and reléeuing the earle of Champaigne in such bountifull wise in his necessitie, that he was readie to forsake the French kings seruice, and cleaue to king Richard. But howsoeuer it came to passe, partlie through enuie (as hath béene thought) conceiued at the great déeds of king Richard, whose mightie power and valiantnesse he could not well abide, and partlie for other respects him moouing, he tooke the sea with thrée gallies of the Geneuois, and returned into Italie, and so home into France, hauing promised first vnto king Richard at his departure out of the holie land, and after to pope Celestine at Rome, that he would [232]not attempt any hurtfull enterprise against the English dominions, till king Richard should be returned foorth of the The euill dealling & breach of promise of the French king.holie land. But this promise was not kept, for after that he was returned into France, he first sought to procure the foresaid erle John, king Richards brother, to rebell against him, promising him not onelie aid to reduce all his brothers dominions into his hands, but also to giue his sister Adela in marriage, whom king Richard vpon suspicion of vnchast liuing, had forsaken, as before ye haue heard. But when earle John was dissuaded by his mother, from accepting this offer (which otherwise as it is said he would willinglie haue receiued) king Philip still reteined a malicious rancor in his hart, and in reuenge of old displeasures, would haue attempted the warre against the subiects of king Richard, if his lords would haue ioined with him: but they considering what slander would redound hereby both to him and them for the iniurie doone to the christian common-welth, in making warre against him that was occupied in defense of the faith against the common enimies of christendome, would not giue their consent thereto, and so the matter rested, till king Richard was taken prisoner in Almaigne, and then what followed, it shall after appeare.

Wil. Paruus. Enuious discord among the christians.In the meane while, the christian armie atchiued some worthie enterprises in the holie land, though not manie, by reason of such enuious discord as reigned amongst the chéefe gouernours. It chanced yet on the éeue of the Natiuitie of our ladie next after the departure of king Philip, as king Richard marched foorth towards Japh ancientlie called Joppa, that the Soldan Saladine taking aduantage of the place, K. Richard discomfiteth the Saracens néere to Port Japh.did set vpon the rereward of the christians: but his Saracens (after they had fought right fiercelie from noone till sunne setting) were so beaten backe at length, and repelled with such losse and disaduantage, that in 40. yeares before they had not susteined at one time greater damage. Amongst other of the christians slaine at that encounter, was one James Dauenes, a man of high prowesse and valiancie.

*Rog. Houed.*Moreouer, king Richard wan diuerse townes and castels out of the enimies hands, as Ascalon, Darus, and diuerse other, and some he fortified, as Ascalon aforesaid, and Port Japh, otherwise called Joppa. There were sundrie encounters also betwixt the Saracens and christians, wherein king Richard and his people bare themselues so manfullie, that the victorie for the most part continuallie rested on their side. At one 1192.time also, hearing of a great conueie of vittels, munitions, and other things which came from Babylon towards Jerusalem to furnish Saladine and his armie (which conueies they call carauannes) king Richard with a competent power of men met them on the waie, and distressed those that were attendant vpon the safegard of that carriage, being in number about two thousand horssemen, besides a great multitude of footmen, and therewith tooke the carriages with foure thousand and six hundred camels and dromedaries, besides an innumerable sort of mules, asses, and other beasts of burthen.

¶ But to speake of all the worthie exploits atchiued by king Richard and his valiant capteins there in the holie land against the infidels, it would require a long treatise, and therefore here we passe them ouer. This is to be noted, that amongst other of whom we find honorable mention made by writers for their high valiancie shewed in those The names of such noble men as were famous for their valiant dooings in this voiage.exploits, these are named as cheefe, Robert earle of Leicester, Hubert bishop of Salisburie, with the earles of S. Paule and Dreux, beside diuerse other, as Hugh de Gourney, William de Borrez, Walcline de Ferrers, Roger de Toonie, James de Auenes, the bishop of Beauuois, William de Barres, William de Tarland, Drogo de Merlo, Robert de Nealle, Henrie Fitz Nicholas, Robert de Newburg, Rafe de S. Marie, Arnold de Bois, Henrie de Mailoc, William & Saule de Bruil, Andrew de Chauignie, Henrie de Graie, Peter de Pratellis, Stephan de Turneham, Baldwin Carron, Clarenbald de Mount Chablon, Manser de Lisle, Richard de Orques and Theodorike Philip, Ferrike de Vienne, Gilbert Malemaine, Alexander d'Arsie, Stephan de Longchamp, Seguin de Barret, Roger de Glanuille, Raimond Fitz Prince, Bartholomew de Mortimer, Gerard Furniuall, Rafe de De Poole aliàs de Stagno.Malleon, Roger de Sacie, William de Poole, Hugh de Neuill, Henrie Teutch or (if ye will) Teutonicus [233]the kings standardbearer, with diuerse others, as well Englishmen, Frenchmen, Normans, Poictouins, Aniouines, Britans, Gascoignes, as other nations, of whome partlie mention is alreadie made before in this booke, and partlie for breefenesse diuerse are omitted.

But now to returne, sure it is, that king Richard meant to haue recouered the citie of Jerusalem, and all the holie land out of the Saracens hands, by the assistance of almightie God: if the doubt which he had of his brother the earle of Mortaigns practises, & the French kings doings, which were brought to him with a greeuous report, had not *Galf. Vinsaf.*reuoked him home. For diuerse messengers were sent dailie into the holie land, to aduertise him of such dangers as were like to insue, if by his speedie returne the same were not preuented. And first after Easter, there came to him the prior of Hereford with letters from the bishop of Elie, conteining a sore information against his brother earle John, for hauing expelled those whom he had appointed rulers ouer the realme of England, and altered the state of things there contrarie to the ordinances by him deuised afore his setting forward vpon his iournie (as before ye haue partlie heard.)

Vpon receipt of which letters, he meant immediatlie at the first to haue returned, and to haue left behind him a conuenient power of men, to wit, thrée hundred knights or men of armes, and two thousand chosen footmen, to abide vpon the defense of the holie land, with other christians at his costs and charges. But yet at length he was persuaded to tarrie, speciallie till things were set in some better staie, which were out of The marques of Montferrato murthered by the Assassini.order by the death of the marques of Montferrato, lord of Tire, whom two traitorous Saracens of the kind which they name Assassini had murthered. After whose death Henrie earle of Champaigne nephue to king Richard married his wife, and was made king of Jerusalem, Guido resigning to him his title, vnto whome as it were in recompense king Richard gaue the Ile of Cypres: although some write, that the knights Templers had bought it of him before. Thus king Richard remaining still in the holie land, shortlie after Whitsuntide, there came an other messenger to him, one John de Alanzon a clearke, bringing worsse newes out of England than the prior of Hereford had brought before, which in effect conteined, that Earle John purposed to seize vpon the kingdom in his brothers absence.his brother earle John was alied as a confederat with the French king, and meant through his setting on, to seize into his possession the whole realme of England, notwithstanding the persuasion of his mother quéene Elianor and other his fréends to the contrarie.

Herevpon king Richard was fullie persuaded to returne home, but yet William de Poicters K. Richards chapleine.through the admonition of certeine persons, and namelie of one William de Poicters, a chapleine of his, he eftsoones altered his purpose, and so remained there, till at length through enuie and malice still increasing amongst the Christians, he perceiued how no good purpose go forward, since that which séemed good to some, was misliked of other; and speciallie our writers put great blame in the French men, who either vpon disdaine or other displeasure would not be persuaded to follow their aduise, which were knowne best to vnderstand the state of things in those parties. And herevpon, when the armie was aduanced to Betenoble, a place not past foure leagues distant from Jerusalem, bicause their mind might not be fulfilled for the besieging of Jerusalem, which they had intended to take in hand (whereas the residue would rather that they shuld haue gone to besiege Babylon in Aegypt, and that vpon sundrie great respects) the Frenchmen raised their field, and returned againe to Acres in great despite, putting the rest of the armie also (so much as in them laie) in danger of vtter ruine and distresse.

An. Reg. 4.Then king Richard and the other Christian capteins perceiuing how the matter inclined, and giuing ouer all hope of any more good successe, followed them. So that after they were thus returned to Acres, king Richard still doubting least his long absence from home might put him in danger of more losse here, than he saw hope of present gaine to be had there, in such diuersitie of humours and priuie malice which reigned among them, he determined fullie to depart homewards, with no lesse purpose to returne thither againe after he had setled things at home in such sure stay as was expedient for the suertie of [234]his owne estate and quietnesse of his people. Herevpon being readie to enter into his ships *Wil. Paruus*.at Acres [or as some haue, being on his iournie homewards in Cypres] he was aduertised that the Souldane Saladine had taken the town of Japh, slaine a great number of the christians within it, and besieged the residue within the castell, the which (constreined through feare) had compounded to yéeld, if within thrée daies there came no succour.

King Richard being hereof aduertised, and turning gréef into valiancie, with all spéed sailed backe vnto Japh, and landing there with his people, caused his enimies to forsake the towne: but anon assembling themselues againe togither, they turned once more to besiege it, wherevpon he issued foorth into the fields, and fought with them sundrie K. Richard rescueth Port Japh.daies togither, till finallie they were content to forsake their enterprise, and to depart thence for altogither. In these conflicts the valiant courage of King Richard, and the worthie manhood of his souldiers right well appeared: *Rad. Niger. Matth. Paris.*for he brought not with him at that time vnto Japh aboue 80 men of armes, and foure hundred other souldiers with crossebowes, and yet with that small handfull of men, and some aid of them that he found there in the castell, he did not onelie bid battell to the enimies, which were numbered to 62 thousand, but also put them to the woorsse, and caused them to flee backe, to their great shame and confusion.

Cephas. K. Richard fell sicke.Thus Japh being deliuered out of the enimies hands, king Richard fell sicke at a castell called Cephas, and so remained there certeine daies, till he had recouered his health. In which meane time the Soldane Saladine seeming to lament his case, sent vnto him certeine of his councellors to common with him of peace, declaring that although he well vnderstood that king Richard ment shortlie to returne into his countrie, and that after his departure out of the east parts, he could with small adoo recouer all that the christians yet held within the holie land, he would neuerthelesse in respect of king Richards high prowes, and noble valliancie, grant a peace for a certeine time, so that not onelie Ascalon, but also all other such townes and places as the christians had fortified or woone since the conquest of Acres should be raced, as touching their walles, bulworks, gates, and other fortifications.

King Richard (though he perceiued that this offer of peace tended vnto this point cheefelie, that Saladine would thereby adnihilate whatsoeuer the christian armie had doone in the holie land since his & the French kings arriuall, so that by the said peace he should gaine more than by the edge of his sword) did somewhat staie at this offer and demand, as a thing greatlie dishonourable to the christians, to lose by treatie of peace so much or rather more than they got by force of warres (a meere token of faint and féeble courage) yet considering that in such necessitie both of his departure from thence, and also of lacke of other succors to resist the puissance of the enimies, after his comming awaie, he iudged it best to take the offer at the enimies hands in auoiding of A peace concluded betwixt the Christians & Saracens.some greater euill. Herevpon therefore was a peace concluded to endure for thrée yeares, thrée moneths, thrée wéeks, thrée daies, and three houres, to begin at Easter next insuing. And among other articles, it was couenanted, that the christians should haue frée passage to come and go vnto the citie of Ierusalem, to visit the holie sepulchre there, which was granted; so that amongst a great number of christians thatHubert bishop of Salisburie.presentlie vpon this conclusion went thither, Hubert bishop of Salisburie was one, who had continued about the king during the time of all his iournie till this time.

King Richard hauing thus concluded with Saladine, tooke the sea, and comming againe into Cypres, sent his wife queene Berengaria with his sister Ioane (late quéene of Sicile) into England by the long seas, but K. Richard taketh his iornie homewards.he himselfe not minding to lie long on the seas, determined to take his course into Grecia, and so by land to passe homewards with all speed possible. Howbeit yer he could atteine his purpose, his chance was to be driuen by tempest into the coast of Istria, not farre from Aquilia, where he stood in some doubt of his life. For if he had beene knowne and taken, they would surelie haue killed him, [235]bicause of the slander that K. Richard slandered for the death of ye marques of Montferrato.went of him, as guiltie of the death of Conrade the marquesse of Montferrato, who indéed was slaine by two of the Assassini in the citie of Tyrus, whilest king Richard was in the holie land (as before yée haue heard.)

He therefore hauing here made shipwracke, and doubting to fall into the hands of any person in those parts that bare good will vnto the marquesse (against whome he had indeed shewed himselfe not fréendlie in a quarrell betwixt the said marquesse and Guido king of Ierusalem) made the best shift he could to get away, yet knowledge being had of him, and *W. Paruus.* Erle of Gorze Saltzburge.serch made after him by one Meinard of Gorezein, he lost eight of his seruants, and so came to a towne within the bishoprike of Saltzburge called Frisake, where he was eftsoones in danger to haue beene taken againe by one Frederike de saint Soome, who notwithstanding tooke six of his men, but yet he himselfe with three other of his companie made shift K. Richard commeth to Vienna.to get away. Finallie comming to Vienna in Austrich, and there causing his seruants to prouide meat for him, more sumptuous and fine than was thought requisit for so meane a person as he counterfeited then to beare out in countenance, it was streightwaies suspected that he was some*Polydor.*other maner of man than he pretended, and in fine, those that marked more diligentlie the maner of him, perceiued what he was, and gaue knowledge to the duke of Austrich named Leopold, being then in the citie of Vienna, what they had scene. His page that had the Dutch toong, going about the towne to change gold, and buy vittels, bewraied him, hauing by chance the kings gloues vnder his girdle: wherevpon comming to be examined for feare of tortures confessed the truth.

*Ra. Niger.*The duke streightwaies caused the house where he was lodged, to be set about with armed men, and sent other into the house to apprehend him. He being warie that he was descried, got him to his weapon: but they aduising him to be contented, and alledging the dukes commandement, he boldlie answered, "that sith he must be taken, he being a king, would yéeld himselfe to none of the companie but to the duke alone, and therefore if it would please him to come, he would yéeld himselfe into K. Richard submitteth himselfe to the duke of Austrich.his hands." The duke hearing of this, spéedilie came vnto him, whom he meeting, deliuered vp his sword, and committed him vnto his custodie. The duke reioising of such a preie, brought him vnto his palace, and with gentle words enterteined him, though he meant no great good towards him, as well inough appeared in that he committed him to the keeping of certeine gentlemen, which without much courtesie looked streightlie inough to him for starting awaie, in somuch that they kept him in cold irons (as some authours doo write.) He was taken after the maner *N. Triuet.*aforesaid in December vpon S. Thomas éeue, in the yéere of our Lord 1192. and in the fourth yeare of his reigne.

*Polychron.*The duke of Austrich owght the king no good will, bicause he had cast downe his ensignes pitcht vp in a turret at Acres, which he had woone at the verie time

31

when that citie was deliuered by the Saracens: for while they were in tretie on the one side, the duke on the other, not knowing The cause of the displeasure betwixt the duke of Austrich & king Richard.anie thing thereof, gaue the assault vnto that part of the towne which was appointed vnto him to besiege. And so being entred the towne, and perceiuing that by treatie it was to be deliuered, he retired into the turret which he had first woone and entred, and there set vp his standard and ensignes, which king Richard (as the Dutch writers affirme) comming thither, threw downe and trode vnder his féet.

*Ger. Dor.*But Geruasius Dorobornensis declareth this matter somewhat otherwise, as thus. After that the said citie of Acres was rendred into the christian mens hands (saith he) diuerse lords tooke their lodgings as they thought good, and hanged foorth their ensignes. And as it chanced, the duke of Austrich placing himselfe in one of the fairest palaces of all the citie, put foorth his ensigne, whereof king Richard being warie, came thither with a companie of hardie souldiers about him, and threw downe the dukes ensigne, so displacing him out of that so pleasant and *Rog. Houed.*beautifull a lodging. For this cause, and also surmizing that king Richard should be guiltie of the death of the marques Conrade, the duke of Austrich shewed such discourtesie towards him. But concerning the murther of[236]the marques, the chéefe gouernour of those Saracens called Assassini cleared king Richard by a letter written and directed vnto the duke of Austrich in manner as followeth.

A letter directed to the duke of Austrich, wherein king Richard is cleared of the death of the marquesse of Mountferrat, whereof he was vehementlie suspected.

Lvpoldo duci Austriæ, Vetus de Monte salutem. Cùm plurimi reges & principes vltra mare Richardum regem Angliæ & dominum de morte marchisi inculpent, iuro per dominum qui regnat in æternum, & per legem quam tenemus, quòd in eius mortem nullam culpam habuit. Est siquidem causa mortis ipsius marchisi talis. Vnus ex fratribus nostris in vnam nauem de Satalei, ad partes nostras veniebat, & tempestas illum fortè ad Tyrum appulit, & marchisus fecit illum capere & occidere, & magnam pecuniam eius rapuit. Nos verò marchiso nuncios nostros misimus, mandantes vt pecuniam fratris nostri nobis redderet, & de morte fratris nostri nobiscum se concordaret, & noluit.

Nec non & nuncios nostros spreuit, & mortem fratris nostri super Reginaldum dominum de Sidonis posuit, & nos tantùm fecimus per amicos nostros, quod in veritate scimus, quòd ille fecit illum occidere & pecuniam rapere. Et iterum alium nuncium nostrum nomine Edrisum misimus ad eum, quem in mare mergere voluit, sed amici nostri illum à Tyro festinanter fecerunt recedere, qui ad nos peruenit, & ista nobis nunciauit. Nos quoque ex illa hora marchisum desiderauimus occidere. Túncque duos fratres misimus ad Tyrum, qui eum apertè & ferè coram omni populo Tyri occiderunt.

Hæc ergò fuit causa mortis marchisi, & benè dicimus vobis in veritate, quòd dominus Richardus rex Angliæ in hac marchisi morte nullam culpam habuit. Et qui propter hoc domino regi Angliæ malum fecerunt, iniustè fecerunt, & sine causa. Sciatis pro certo, quòd nullum hominem huius mundi pro mercede aliqua vel pecunia occidimus, nisi priùs nobis malum fecerit. Et sciatis quòd has literas fecimus in domo nostra ad castellum nostrum Messiat in dimidio Septembri, anno ab Alexandro 1505.

The same in English.

Vetus de Monte to Lupold duke of Austrich sendeth greeting. Where manie kings and princes beyond the seas blame Richard king of England of the marques his death, I sweare by the lord that reigneth euerlastinglie, and by the law which we hold, that he was not in fault for his death. For the verie cause of the marques his death was such as followeth. One of our brethren in a ship of Satalie came towards our parties, and chanced by tempest to be driuen vnto Tyre, and the marques caused him to be taken and slaine and tooke a great portion of monie that he had in the ship with him. Whervpon we sent our messengers to the marques, commanding him to restore vnto vs the monie of our brother, and to compound with vs for our said brothers death, and he would not.

Moreouer, he also contemned our messengers, & laid the fault of our brothers death vpon Reginald lord of Sidon, and we did so much through our freends, that we got full vnderstanding that the marques himselfe caused him to be slaine, and tooke his monie. And therefore we sent vnto him againe an other messenger named Edrisus, whome he would haue drowned in the sea, but our freends made such shift, that they procured him to depart with speed from Tyre, who returned to vs, and signified these things to vs for certeine. And from that houre euer after we had a desire to slea the marques: and so [237]then we sent two of our brethren vnto Tyre, who openlie, & in a manner in presence of all the people of Tyre slue him.

This therefore was the verie cause of the death of the marques: & we say to you in good sooth, that the lord Richard king of England, in this death of the marques was nothing culpable: and they that haue doone anie displeasure vnto the king of England for this cause, they haue doone it wrongfullie, and without anie iust occasion. Know ye for certeine, that we do not vse to kill anie man of this world for anie bribe, or for monie, except he haue doone to vs some harme afore time. And know ye that we haue made these letters in our house at our castell of Messuat, in the midst of September, in the yeare from Alexander the great, 1505.

¶ Thus we see how king Richard was cleared of that crime concerning the marques his death by the tenour of this letter. And verelie it is most like that king Richard would haue béene loth to haue communicated his purpose vnto such a wicked kind of pagans as the Assassini were, if he had pretended any such matter, but rather would haue sought his reuenge by some other meanes. Now therefore to our purpose.

The newes of the taking of king Richard was anon bruted and blowne ouer all Germanie, wherevpon the emperour Henrie the sixt, the sonne of 1193.Frederike the first, sent in all hast vnto the duke, persuading him to deliuer the king into his hands, being able to susteine and abide the malice of all them that would be offended with the taking and deteining of him prisoner, as the pope and others. The emperour well vnderstood the wealth and riches of England, and therefore hoped to make some good purchase by ransoming the king, if he might get him out of the dukes hands. The duke perceiuing also the emperours meaning, durst not well denie his request, and therefore he deliuered the king vnto them that The king is deliuered to the emperor. *Matth. Paris.*were sent from the emperour, who couenanted to giue vnto the said duke the summe of 6000. pounds of Cullen weight for the hauing of the said king. The emperour thus receiuing the king at the hands of the duke of Austrich, commanded that he should be committed to close prison, and would not doo so much as once speake with him. This he did, to cause the king vpon an indignation and wearinesse of that maner of life, to make speed in offering some large masse of monie for his libertie & deliuerance. ¶ Thus we sée how couetousnesse infected the hearts of the mightie, and what occasion the emperour and duke did take, to inrich themselues by the meanes of the king, whome they forced not to impouerish, so their owne greedie worme were serued. But this hath béene a disease not so generall as ancient, according to his words that said,

*Ouid. lib. Fast. 1.*Vix ego Saturno quenquam regnante videbam,Cuius non animo dulcia lucra forent.

*Rog. Houed.*Here is to be remembred by the waie, that about the same time, or somewhat before, in the yeare of our Lord 1192. the pope sent two legats Two legats from ye pope.(namelie, Octauian bishop of Hostia, and Jordane de Fossa noua) into Normandie, to reconcile the bishop of Elie and the archbishop of Rouen: but comming vnto Gisors, they were staied from entring any further into Normandie interdicted.the countrie, wherevpon they did interdict the whole duchie of Normandie, togither with William Fitz Radulfe lord steward of that countrie, bicause he was the man that had so staied them. Immediatlie herevpon, queene Elianor, and the archbishop of Rouen sent vnto those legats Hugh bishop of Durham, requiring them to release that sentence of interdiction so pronounced against the steward and countrie of Normandie in the kings absence, but they would not, except they might be receiued into Normandie: howbeit, the pope being sent vnto, released it, and caused the legats to release it also, and yet they entred not into Normandie at all.

The earle of Pieregort & others wast the K. of Englands lands.This yeare, whilest the seneschall of Gascoigne laie sicke, the earle of Pieregort, and the vicount of March, and almost all the lords and barons of Gascoigne, began to waste and destroie the lands of king Richard. And though the seneschall manie times by messengers required a peace, or at the least some truce, yet could he not haue any grant [238]thereof: wherfore vpon his recouerie of health The seneschal of Gascoigne reuengeth iniurie.he inuaded the lands of the said earle, tooke the castels and fortresses and some of them he fortified, and kept to the kings vse, and some of them he raced downe to the ground. He also inuaded the vicounts countrie, and subdued it to the kings gouernement. Shortlie after came the brother of the The king of Nauarres brother.king of Nauarre, with eight hundred knights or men of armes to the seneschals aid, and so they two togither entring into the lands of the earle of Tholouse, tooke diuerse castels and fortresses within the same, of the which some they fortified, and some they raced, and rode euen to the gates of Tholouse, and lodged in maner vnder the walles of the citie.

A little before Christmas also, diuerse of those that had béene in the holie land with king Richard, came home into England, not knowing but that king Richard had beene at home before them, and being asked where they thought he was become, they could say no more but that they had seene the ship wherein he first went aboord, arriuing at Brendize in Puglia. At length, when newes came that he was taken and staied as prisoner, the archbishop of Rouen and other the rulers of the realme of The abbats of Boxley and Roberts-bridge.England, sent the abbat of Boxeley and the abbat of Roberts-bridge with all spéed into Almaine to speake with him, and to vnderstand his state, and what his pleasure was in all things. Who comming to Germanie, passed through the countrie into Baierland, where at a place called Oxefer they found the king as then on his iournie towards the emperour, to whom (as yée haue heard) the duke of Austrich did send him. The said abbats attended him to the emperours court, and remained there with him till the emperour and he were accorded, in manner as after shall be shewed: and then after Easter they returned with the newes into England.

*Ger. Dor.*Vpon report hereof order was taken for manie things, but cheefelie for the state: in which dealings, forsomuch as those which had the rule of the land stood in great doubt of things (for the inconstant nature of earle John was of them much suspected) first they caused a new oth of allegiance to be made to king Richard, and receiued of the people. They fortified also such townes and castels as were of importance, both with repairing the walles and other defenses about the same, and furnishing them with men, munition and vittels. Thus was the land brought into some order.

The French king counselleth K. John to vsurpe against his brother.In the meane while, the French king being aduertised that king Richard was deteined as prisoner reioised not a little thereat, and with all speed by secret messages did send for his brother earle John, who was readie to come at his call. And being come, he exhorted him not to suffer so conuenient an occasion to passe, but to take the gouernement of the realme of England now into his hands, promising him all such aid as he could of him reasonablie require: with other like talke still tending to the prouocation of the earle to forsake his allegiance vnto his brother. And to say the truth, earle John was easilie persuaded so to doo, and therefore vpon his immediat returne into England, assembled an armie, and with the same (and such strangers as he brought with him) began to prooue maisteries, first winning the castels of Windsore, Wallingford, Notingham, and diuerse other, and fortifieng the same to his owne vse and defense.

The barons of the land, iudging such vnlawfull doings not to be anie longer suffered, first besieged the castell of Windsore, and after preparing to leuie a greater force, did put them within in such feare, that they yéelded vp the same, séeking to escape by flight, some into one place, and some into an other, the which yet being apprehended were *Ger. Dor.*put to worthie execution. But this was not doone without continuance of time, & without great trouble & charges to the realme: for whereas there was a practise betwixt the French king and earle John, that a great power of strangers, & namelie Flemings should haue come into the realme (for whose transporting a great number of ships were brought togither at Witsand) yet the high prouidence and goodnesse of God disappointed their purpose. For their messengers being taken which were sent hither into England, the treason was reuealed, and by the queene mothers appointment (who cheefelie then ruled the land) a great companie of knights, men of armes, and commons of the countrie, [239]watched the sea coasts ouer against Flanders, to keepe the enimies from landing. They began thus to watch in the passion wéeke, and so continued till a certeine time after Easter. Howbeit earle John came secréetlie ouer, in hope to haue not onelie the assistance of the Welshmen and of manie other his freends in England, but also of the Scots, howbeit, the king of Scots would not meddle. He therefore with such Welshmen and other as he had brought ouer, and such Englishmen as he could get to take his part, began such attempts (as before ye haue heard) to the disquieting of the whole realme, and great displeasure of the king.

Moreouer, beside that power of the barons which laid siege to Windsor castell, there were Noble men also in other parts of the realme that The archbishop of Yorke. Hugh Bardolfe. William de Stuteuille.were readie to resist him. And amongst other, Geffrey the archbishop of Yorke, with Hugh Bardolfe one of the kings iustices, and William de Stuteuille, assembled an armie, and comming to Doncaster, fortified[9] the towne: but when the archbishop would haue gone forward to besiege the castell of Tickhill, which earle John had in possession, the other two his associats would not consent to go with him, bicause they were seruants, and reteined with earle John. Herewith the archbishop being sore offended, departed from them, calling them traitors to their king, and enimies to the realme.

About the same time did the French king enter into Normandie with an armie, & comming to the towne of Gisors, besieged it, the which one Gilbert de Vascoll or Guascoill capteine thereof (to his high reproch) yéelded vp vnto him, with an other castell also called Nefle, which he *Wil. Paruus*.had likewise in kéeping. After this, the French king entring into the countrie of Veuxine or Veulquessine, wan diuers towns and fortresses in the same, and passing forward, tooke Val de Rueil, and Neusburge, and Rouen besieged. The earle of Leicester.finallie comming before the citie of Rouen he laid siege thereto: but the earle of Leicester being gotten into the citie before the French kings comming thither, so incouraged the citizens, that they stoutlie standing to their defense, caused the French king to his great dishonour to raise his field, hauing lost there more than he wan. Yet to saue *Polydor*.other townes and castels from taking, and the countrie from destruction, the rulers of the same procured a truce for a great summe of monie, which they couenanted to giue, deliuering vp foure notable castels by waie of engagement, till the summe agreed vpon should be to him contented and dulie paid.

In the meane time, earle John as head of all the conspiratours, perceiuing himselfe not able to atchieue his purpose as then, nor to resist the lords and barons of the realme, being vp in armour against him, and now growen to greater stomach, bicause they vnderstood by the bishop of Salisburie latelie arriued, of the kings welfare, and hope of deliuerance; and furthermore, considering that he was disappointed both of Scots and Flemings as he had well hoped should haue come to his aid: he tooke a truce with the lords of the kings side, by the earnest Michaelmas, saith*Ger. Dorob*.trauell of the bishop of Salisburie, till the feast of All saincts, so as the castels of Windsore, Wallingford, and the Peake, should remaine in the hands of his mother queene Elianor; but the castels of Notingham and Tickhill remained still in his owne possession, the which with such other castels as he held within the land, he furnished with garrisons of his owne men and freends, and then went againe ouer into France to the French king, to purchase some new aid at his hands according to his promise.

Wil. Paruus.Here will we leaue earle John conferring with the French king, and returne to the king of England. Vpon Palmesundaie after that he was deliuered (or rather betraied) into the emperours hands, he was brought The emperour chargeth king Richard with iniuries doone to the Sicilians.before the princes and lords of the empire, in whose presence the emperour charged him with diuerse vnlawfull dooings: and namelie picked a quarell at him for the wrongs and hurts doone to the Sicilians in time of his soiourning in their Ile, as he went towards the holie land. For albeit the said emperour had nothing as then to doo in the countrie, yet for somuch as he had latelie recouered the Ile of Sicile out of king Tancreds hands, and was now intituled king thereof by the pope, in right of [240]his wife Constance, the daughter of Roger king of Sicile, and so by reason therof seemed to be gréeuouslie offended with him for his dooings about the recouering of the monie from Tancred, which neuerthelesse was iustlie due vnto his sister for her dowrie, as in the processe afore I *W. Paruus. Matth. West*.The kings wisdome in making his answere.haue alreadie declared. King Richard notwithstanding these vaine and other friuolous obiections laid to his charge, made his answears alwaies so pithilie and directlie to all that could be laid against him, and excused himselfe in euerie point so not onelie greatlie commended him for the same, but from thenceefoorth vsed him more courteouslie, and suffered that his fréends might haue accesse to him more fréelie than before they could be permitted.

*Polydor.*The pope also being aduertised of the taking of king Richard, was much offended, that anie Christian prince, hauing taken vpon him the defense of the Christian faith against the infidels, should be so vsed in his returne from so godlie an enterprise: and therefore sent both to the duke of Austrich, and to the emperour, requiring them to set him at libertie. But the emperour declared plainlie that he would be answered for such summes of monie as king Richard had taken out of Sicile before he would release him or set him at libertie.

The bishop of Salisburie sent into England.When king Richard perceiued that no excuses would serue, though neuer so iust, but that he must néeds paie to his couetous host some great summe of monie for his hard interteinment, he sent the bishop of Salisburie into England, to take order with the barons of the realme to prouide for the paiment of his ransome, which bishop (as yée haue heard) after the peace concluded with Saladine, went vnto Ierusalem to visit the holie sepulchre, and now comming into Sicile, as he returned homewards, had knowledge there how king Richard was taken prisoner in Austrich, and remained in the emperours hands: wherevpon he turned that waie foorth, and comming to him, was now sent into England with commission (as I haue said) to leauie monie for the kings ransome. He landed here the twentith day of Aprill, by whose comming the land was the sooner brought in *Ger. Dor.*quiet: for the agréement which earle John tooke (as before yée haue heard) was chéefelie procured by his meanes. For till his comming, the castell of Windsore was not woone, the siege being but slackelie followed by the archbishop of Rouen, who had diuerse of his fréends within it, and therefore was not verie earnest against them.

Rog. Houed. The bishop of Elie commeth to the king.When the bishop of Salisburie was departed towards England, the bishop of Elie came to the king and trauelled so earnestlie betwixt the emperour and him, that finallie the emperour (partlie through his suit, & partlie for that he had béene verie much called vpon by the pope and other for his deliuerie) tooke order with him for the redéeming of his The emperor agréeth with king Richard for his ransome. *N. Triuet.Matth. Paris.*libertie, and appointed what summe he should pay for his ransome, which (as some write) was two hundred thousand markes: other saie that it was but 140 thousand marks of the poise of Cullen weight. But William Paruus, who liued in those daies, affirmeth it was one hundred thousand pounds, and Roger Houeden saith an hundred thousand marks of Cullen poise, to be paid presentlie at the kings first comming into England, and fiftie thousand marks afterwards, that is to say, thirtie thousand to the emperour, and twentie thousand to the duke of Austrich, as it were in recompense of the iniurie done to him in the holie land; where king Richard ouerthrew his ensignes: and for the same to deliuer sufficient suerties.

R. Houed. Lands assigned to king Richard.Moreouer, we find in Roger Houeden that the emperour amongst other the articles of this agréement thus concluded betwixt him and king Richard, gaue and granted, and by his letters patents confirmed vnto him these lands hereafter mentioned, that is to saie: Prouance with the citie of Vienne, and Viennois, the citie of Marseils, Narbon, Arles and Lion vpon the Rhone, with the countrie vp to the Alps, and all those possessions which belonged to the empire in Burgoine, with the homages of the king of Aragon and of the earle of S. Giles: wherein is to be noted, that with the precinct of the premisses thus granted to king Richard, fiue archbishops sées, and thirtie three bishops sées are included. Howbeit the truth is, that the emperour neuer had possession of these countries, cities, [241]and towns himselfe, neither would the inhabitants receiue any person so by him appointed to their lord and gouernour, wherefore the king made small account of that his so large grant. But after he once vnderstood the certeintie of the summe that he should paie for his ransome (which businesse he most attended) he sent one with letters by and by and in great hast into England to his treasurers, requiring them *Polydor.*with all conuenient spéed to prouide monie, and to send it to him by a day, that he might be set at libertie with spéed.

Rog. Houed.

Order taken for leuieng monie to paie the kings ransome.These letters being come to the quéene mother, and other that had charge in gouernance of the realme, tooke order that all maner of persons as well spirituall as temporall, should giue the fourth part of their whole reuenues to them for that yeare accrewing, and as much more of their mooueable goods, and that of euerie knights fée there should be leuied the sum of twentie shillings. Also that the religious houses of the orders of the Cisteaux and Sempringham should giue all their wools for that yeare towards the kings ransome.

The hard dealing of officers in the collection. Now those that had commission to leuie this monie, being poisoned with couetousnesse, and incensed with a gréedie desire (than the which as the poet saith,

———— nulla est hac maior Erinnys, Hanc memorant Acheronte satam, per tristia DitisRegna truces agitare faces, &c.)

vsed much streightnesse in exacting it, not onelie leuieng it to the vttermost value and extent of mens lands, goods, and possessions, but after their owne willes and pleasures: so that vnder colour of the kings commission, and letters to them directed, there séemed not a tribute or subsidie to be raised, but by some publike proclamation all the goods and substance of the people to be appointed as a prey to the kings officers, whereby it came to passe, that not onelie priuate mens goods, Church iewels. but also the chalices, iewels, and vessels belonging to the church were turned into monie, and a farre greater summe made than was at the first commanded, a great part of the ouerplus being conuerted to the vse of those, through whose hands the receipt passed. There was no priuilege nor freedome allowed to exempt any person or place for being contributorie towards the paiment of this monie. The order of Cisteaux that were neuer charged with any paiment before, were now assessed more déepelie than the rest.

The bishop of Norwich. The bishop of Norwich lamenting the iniurious dealings of the pettie officers, and pittieng the people of the church, collected halfe the value of all the chalices within his diocesse himselfe, and to make vp the other halfe of the whole summe, he spared not to giue a great The abbat of saint Albons. portion of his owne treasure. The abbat of S. Albons acquitted all those churches within the compasse of his iurisdiction, by the gift of an hundred marks. But the The bishop of Chester. bishop of Chester had verie ill lucke with his collections; for hauing gathered a great summe of monie to the kings vse, he was spoiled thereof in one night, as he lodged neere vnto Canturburie, being vpon his iournie towards the king. And bicause Matthew de Cléere. Matthew de Cléere that laie in the castell of Douer was knowne to aid those that robbed the said bishop, the archbishop of Canturburie pronounced him accurssed.

R. Houed. The bishop of Elie. About this time, and on the morrow after the natiuitie of saint John Baptist, the bishop of Elie lord chancellour arriued in England, not shewing himselfe in any statelie port (for he tooke vpon him neither the dignitie of chancellour nor legat, nor yet of iustice) but onelie as a simple bishop and messenger sent from the king. The quéene mother, the archbishop of Rouen, and such other as had gouernment of the land, hearing of his comming, met him at saint Albons, where he shewed to them the emperours letters, conteining the agreement made betwixt him and king Richard, and withall appointed certeine lords & barons to go with him at his returne backe to the king, as Gilbert bishop of Rochester, Sifrid bishop of Chichester, Bennet abbat of Peterborow, Richard earle of Clare, Roger Bigot earle of Norfolke, Geffrey de Saie, and diuerse other. It was also ordeined at this same time, that the monie gathered towards the paiment of the kings ransome should remaine in custodie of Hubert bishop of Salisburie, Richard bishop of [242]London, William earle of Arundell, Hameline earle of Warren, and of the Maior of London, vnder the seales of the quéene mother, and of the archbishop of Rouen.

An. Reg. 5.¶ But sée the hap of things, whilest ech one was thus occupied about the Wil. Paruus. aforesaid monie; it chanced that king Richard was at the point to haue béene deliuered into the hands of his deadlie aduersarie the French king, as hereafter you shall heare, noting by the waie the dangerous estate of princes, the manifold distresses whereinto by sinister fate (as well as the inferior & rascall rout of common drudges) they be driuen. For what greater calamitie, what gréeuouser hartach, what more miserable casualtie could haue happened vnto a bondman, than to be deliuered to and fro from the hand of one enimie to another, to be bought and sold for monie, to stand to the courtesies of forren foes, of a king to become a captiue? whervnto the poet did right well allude, when he said,

*Hor. lib. car. 1. ode 10.*Sæpius ventis agitatur ingensPinus, & celsæ grauiore casuDecidunt turres, feriúntq; summosFulmina montes.

The emperour vpon displeasure conceiued against the bishop of Liege, which latelie had atteined to that benefice contrarie to the emperours The bishop of Liege murthered.pleasure, who wished the same rather to an other person, hired certeine naughtie fellowes to go into France, where the bishop remained for feare of the emperours malice, and there to find meanes traitorouslie to slea him, which they accordinglie did, by reason whereof the duke of Louaigne that was brother to the bishop, and other of his kinsmen, vpon knowledge had thereof, meant to haue made the emperour warre, in reuenge of that murther: insomuch that the emperour, to haue the French kings aid against them, was minded to haue deliuered K. Richard vnto him.

Howbeit after that the matter was taken vp, and a concord made betwixt the emperour and his nobles, he changed his purpose also touching the deliuering ouer of king Richard, who perceiuing that till his ransome were paid (which would amount to the summe of an hundred & fiftie thousand marks) he should not get libertie: and putting great confidence in the dexteritie and diligence of Hubert bishop of Salisburie (whome he sent as ye haue heard into England to deale for the leuieng of the same) he thought good to aduance the same bishop to the metropolitane sée of Canturburie, which had beene vacant euer sithence the decease of archbishop Baldwine, that died (as ye haue heard) in the holie land.

*Wil. Paruus.*Herevpon writing to the bishops of the realme, and to the moonks of Canturburie, he required them to procéed to the election of an archbishop for that see, and withall commended vnto them the foresaid Hubert, as a man most sufficient and méet for that roome. He wrote Hubert bishop of Salisburie elected archbishop of Cāturburie.likewise to the queene to further that matter, and easilie hereby obteined his desire. For shortlie after, the same Hubert was elected by the bishops and moonks, which assembled togither for that purpose. He was the 41 archbishop that gouerned that see: for although Reginold bishop of Bath was elected before him, yet bicause he died yer he was installed, he is not put in the number.

The king being now put in good hope of his spéedie deliuerance, sent into England, willing his mother quéene Elianor, the archbishop of Rouen and others, to come ouer vnto him into Almaine, and in the meane time he Hubert archbishop of Cāturburie, lord chéefe iustice.ordeined Hubert the archbishop of Canturburie to remaine at home as lord cheefe iustice. After this, the emperour with the aduice of the princes of the empire, assigned a day to king Richard, in which he should be deliuered out of captiuitie, which was the mondaie next after the twentith day of Christmasse. Wherevpon king Richard wrote vnto Hubert archbishop of Canturburie in forme as followeth.

[243]

The tenour of king Richards letters to the said archbishop.

Richardus Dei gratia rex Angliæ, & dux Normaniæ & Aquitaniæ, & comes Andigauiæ, venerabili patri nostro in Christo, & amico charissimo Huberto eadem gratia Cantuariensi archiepiscopo salutem & sinceræ dilectionis plenitudinem. Quoniam certiores sumus, quòd liberationem nostram plurimùm desideratis, & quòd liberatio nostra admodum vos lætificat, scripto volumus quòd lætitiae nostræ participes sitis. Inde est quòd dilectioni vestræ dignum duximus significare, dominum imperatorem certum diem liberationis nostræ nobis praefixisse, in die lunæ proxima post vicessimum diem natiuitatis Domini, & die dominica proxima sequenti coronabimur de regno prouinciæ, quod nobis dedit. Vnde mittimus in Angliam literas domini imperatoris super hijs patentes, vobis & cæteris amicis nostris beneuolis. Vos autem interim pro omni posse vestro quos scitis nos diligere, consolari velitis, & quos scitis promotionem nostram desiderare. Teste meipso apud Spiram 22. die Septembris.

The emperour also signified by his letters to the lords of England his resolute determination in this matter, as followeth.

The tenour of the emperours letters to the States of England touching king Richard, and the day of his deliuerance, &c.

Henricus Dei gratia Romanorum imperator, & semper Augustus, dilectis suis archiep. episcopis, comitibus, baronibus, militibus, & vniuersis alijs fidelibus Richardi illustris regis Anglorum gratiam suam & omne bonum. Vniuersitati vestræ duximus intimandum, quòd dilecto amico nostro Richardo illustri regi Anglorum domino vestro certum diem liberationis suæ statuimus, à secunda feria post diem natiuitatis domini in tres septimanas apud Spiram siue apud Berenatiam, & inde in septem dies posuimus ei diem coronationis suæ de regno Prouinciæ, quod ei promisimus: & hoc certum habeatis, & indubitatum, nostri siquidem propositi est, & voluntatis, præfatum dominum vestrum specialem promouere sicut amicum nostrum, & magnificentiùs honorare. Datum apud Theallusam vigilia beati Thomæ Apostoli.

Before this king Richard had sent the bishop of Elie into France vnto his brother earle John, who preuailed so much with him, that he returned into Normandie, and there sware fealtie vnto his brother king Richard, and so was contented to forsake the French king. But whereas king Richard commanded that all such castels and honours as he had giuen to him afore time, should now be restored to him againe, as well those in England, as the other on the further side the sea: such as had the same castels in kéeping would not obeie the kings commandement herein, The kings commandement not obeied.refusing to make restitution of those places, according to the tenour & purport of the kings writ, vnto the said earle of Mortaigne, by reason of which refusall, he returned againe to the French king, and stucke to him. Herevpon the French king gaue vnto him the castels of Dreincourt, and Arques, the which ought to haue béene deliuered vnto the archbishop of Reimes as in pledge, who had trauelled as a meane betwixt the French king to whom he was vncle, and the king of England to whom he was cousine, procuring a meeting for agreement to be had betwixt them at a certeine place betwixt Vaucolur and Tulle in the borders of Lorraine. But notwithstanding all that he could doo, matters were so farre out of frame, and such [244]mistrust was entred into the minds of the parties, that no conclusion held. So that all the hope which king Richard had, was by paiment of his ransome to redéeme his libertie, and then to shift with things as he might. And so finallie when the monie was once readie, or 1194.rather a sufficient portion thereof, the same was conueied ouer into Germanie, and paiment made to the emperour of the more part of the kings ransome, and sufficient pledges left with him for the rest, as the archbishop of Rouen, the bishop of Bath [Baldwin Wac] and other which were of late come out of England to see and salute the king.

Rog. Houed. King Richard released out of captiuitie.Herevpon king Richard, after he had béene prisoner one yeare, six weekes, and thrée daies, was set at libertie on Candlemasse day (as most writers agrée) and then with long and hastie iournies, not kéeping the high waies, he hasted foorth towards England. It is reported that if he had lingred by the way, he had béene eftsoones apprehended. For the emperour being incensed against him by ambassadors that came from the French king, immediatlie after he was set forward, began to repent himselfe in that he had suffered him so soon to depart from him, and herevpon sent men after him with all speed to bring him backe if they could by any meanes ouertake him, meaning as then to haue kept him in perpetuall prison.

R. Houed. The offers of the French K. and erle John to haue the K. of England kept still in prison.Some write that those ambassadours sent from the French king, with other from earle John, came to the emperor before king Richard was deliuered, offering in the French kings name fiftie thousand marks of siluer, and in the name of earle John thirtie thousand, vpon condition that K. Richard might remaine still in captiuitie vntill the feast of S. Michaell next insuing; or else if it might so please him, he should receiue a thousand pounds of siluer for euerie moneth, whilest king Richard should be deteined in his prison, or otherwise fiftie thousand marks of siluer more than the first offer, at one entire paiment, if he would deliuer him into their hands, or at the leastwise to kéepe him prisoner by the terme of one whole yeare.

The emperour hearing of such large offers, and yet hoping for more, contrarie to his promise and letters patents therefore granted, proroged the day in which king Richard should haue béene set at libertie, till Candlemasse after, at which daie he was brought from Haguenaw vnto Spiers, where the emperour had called a councell to intreat further of the matter touching his redemption. Here the emperour shewed the letters which he had receiued from the French king and earle John vnto king Richard, who vpon sight and perusing of the same, was maruellouslie amazed, and began to despaire of all speedie deliuerance.

Indéed the emperour sought delaies vpon a couetous desire of the monie offered by the French king and earle John, but yet such princes and The princes that had vndertaken for the emperor to performe the couenants.great lords as had vndertaken for the emperour, that the couenants and articles on his part agréed vpon in the accord passed betwixt him and king Richard, should be in ech behalfe performed [that is to saie, the archbishops of Ments, Cullen, and Saltzburge, the bishops of Wormes, Spiers, and Liege, the dukes of Suaben, Austrich, & Louain, the Palsgraue of the Rhine, and others] came to the emperour, and reproouing him for his couetous mind, in that he deferred the restoring of king Richard to his libertie, contrarie to the composition, did so much preuaile, that the emperour receiuing pledges for the paiment of the monie yet behind (as before ye haue heard) released king Richard out of captiuitie on the second or (as Roger Houeden saith) the fourth day of Februarie, being a dismall day and an infortunate (as they note them in Robert de Nouant.kalendars.) And where the king would haue left Robert de Nouant the bishop of Couentries brother for a pledge amongst the other, he refused to be one of the number, alledging that he was seruant to earle John. King Richard greeuouslie offended herewith, commanded that he should be apprehended, and committed to prison, & so he was. This Robert was one of those that came with the letters from the French king and earle John to the emperour, about the staieng of king Richards deliuerance.

[245]Furthermore, king Richard the same day in which he was restored to libertie, summoned by his letters Hugh Nouant bishop of Couentrie, to appeare in his court, to answer such things as were to be obiected against him, both before spirituall iudges in that he was a bishop, and also before temporall in that he had holden and exercised a temporall office. On the verie same day also the emperour and the princes of the empire, sent letters vnder their hands and seales to the French king, and to John erle of Mortaigne, commanding them immediatlie vpon sight of the same letters, to restore vnto king Richard all those castels, cities, townes, lands, and other things, which they had taken from him during the time of his remaining in captiuitie, and if they refused thus to doo, then they gaue them to vnderstand by the same letters, that they would aid king Richard to recouer that by force, which had beene wrongfullie taken from him.

Moreouer king Richard gaue and by his deed confirmed vnto sundrie Yéerelie pensions giuen by the king to certeine princes of the empire.princes of the empire for their homage and fealtie, certeine yearelie pensions, as to the archbishop of Ments and Cullen, to the bishop of Liege, to the dukes of Austrich and Louaine, to the marquesse of Mountferrat, to the duke of Meglenburge, Memburge.to the duke of Suaben the emperors brother, to the earle of Bins, to the earle of Holland, and to the sonne of the earle of Henault, of all the which, and other mo, he receiued homage, or rather had their promise by oth to aid him against the French king, which French king, now that he sawe no hope nor likelihood remaining to bring the emperour to the bent of his bowe for the deteining of K. Richard still in captiuitie, raised a power *Wil. Paruus.* The French king inuadeth Normandie.foorthwith, & entring into Normandie (the truce notwithstanding) tooke the towne of Eureux, with diuerse other fortresses thereabouts, and after he had doone mischéefe inough, as it were wearied with[10] euill dooing, he granted eftsoones to stand to the truce, and so returned home.

Finallie after king Richard had dispatched his businesse with the emperour, and the princes of Almaigne, he set forward on his iournie towards England, and hauing the emperours passeport, came to Cullen, where he was ioifullie receiued of the archbishop, the which archbishop attended on him till he came to Antwerpe, where king Richard tooke the water in a gallie that belonged to Alane de Trenchmere, but in the night he went into a ship of Rie, being a verie faire vessell, and so laie *Rog. Houed.*aboord in hir all the night, and in the morning returned to the gallie, and so sailed about the coast, till he came to the hauen of Swin in Flanders, and there staieng fiue daies, on the six day he set foorth He landed the 20. of March being sundaie as R. Houeden[11] and *Rafe de Diceto* write.againe, and at length in good safetie landed at Sandwich the twelfe daie of March, and the morrow after came to Canturburie where he was receiued with procession, as Ger. Dor. saith. From thence he went to Rochester, and on the Wednesday being the sixteenth of March, he came vnto

London, where he was receiued with great ioy and gladnesse of the people, giuing heartie thanks to almightie GOD for his safe returne and deliuerance.

¶ It is recorded by writers, that when such lords of Almaine as came ouer with him, saw the great riches which the Londoners shewed in that triumphant receiuing of their souereigne lord and king, they maruelled greatlie thereat, insomuch that one of them said vnto him; "Surelie oh king, your people are wise and subtile, which do nothing doubt to shew the beautifull shine of their riches now that they haue receiued you home, whereas before they seemed to bewaile their need and pouertie, whilest you remained in captiuitie. For verelie if the emperour had vnderstood that the riches of the realme had bin such, neither would he haue beene persuaded that England could haue béene made bare of wealth, neither yet should you so lightlie haue escaped his hands without the paiment of a more huge and intollerable ransome."

The same yeare that king Richard was taken (as before is mentioned) by the duke of Austrich, one night in the moneth of Januarie about the first watch of the same night, the northwest side of the element appeared of such a ruddie colour as though it had burned, without any clouds or other darknesse to couer it, so that the stars shined through that rednesse, and might be verie well discerned. Diuerse bright strakes appeared to [246]flash vpwards now and then, diuiding the rednesse, thorough the which the stars séemed to be of a bright sanguine colour. In Februarie next insuing, one night after midnight the like woonder was séene, and shortlie after newes came that the king was taken in Almaigne.

On the second daie of Nouember also a little before the breake of the daie, the like thing appeared againe with lesse feare and woonder to the people (than before) being now better accustomed to the like sight againe. And now the same daie and selfe houre that the king arriued at Sandwich, being the second houre of that daie, whilest the sunne shone verie bright and cleare, there appeared a most brightsome and vnaccustomed clearnesse, not farre distant from the sunne, as it were to the length and breadth of a mans personage, hauing a red shining brightnesse withall, like to the rainbow, which strange sight when manie beheld, there were that prognosticated the king alreadie to be arriued.

R. Houed. Diuerse sieges held at one time.In this meane while the bishop of Durham with a great armie besieged the castell of Tickhill; and earle Dauid brother to the king of Scots, with Ranulfe earle of Chester, and earle Ferrers, besieged the castell of Notingham, whilest at the same present the archbishop of Canturburie with a great power besieged Marleburgh castell, the which within a few daies was rendred into his hands, the liues and lims of them within saued. Also the castell of Lancaster was deliuered to him, the which the same archbishops brother had in kéeping vnder earle John, and likewise S. Michaels mount.the abbeie of S. Michaels mount in Cornwall, the which abbeie Henrie de la Pomerey chasing out the moonks, had fortified against the king, and hearing newes of the kings returne home, died (as it was thought) for méere gréefe and feare. These three places were surrendered to the archbishop before the kings returne, but Tickhill & Notingham held out.

King Richard being returned into England, and vnderstanding both how the French king made warre against him in Normandie, and that the state of England was not a little disquieted, by the practise of his brother earle John and his complices, speciallie by reason that diuerse castels were defended by such as he had placed in them, he thought good with all speed to cut off such occasions as might bréed a[12]further mischéefe. The king goeth to Notingham and winneth the castel. Rog. Houed.Wherevpon he first went to Notingham, and within thrée daies after his comming thither (which was on the daie of the Annunciation of our ladie) he constreined them that kept the castell there in his brothers name, to yeeld themselues simplie vnto his mercie, after they had abidden diuerse assaults, by the which euen the first daie the vtter gates were burnt, and certeine defenses destroied, which they had made before the same.

The cheefe of them that were within this castell to defend it were these, William de Vendeuall conestable there, Roger de Mountbegun, Rafe Murdach, Philip de Worceter and Ranulfe de Worceter, brethren. The morow after the surrender was made, the king went to Clipstone, and rode into The forest of Shirewood.the forrest of Shirewood, where he had neuer béene before, the view whereof pleased him greatlie. The castell of Tickhill was likewise at the same time yéelded vnto the bishop of Durham, who receiued it to the kings

41

vse, and them that kept it as prisoners, without anie composition, but standing simplie to the K. mercie. For although those that had these castels in keeping, were sufficientlie prouided of all necessarie things for defense, yet the sudden comming of the king (whom they thought verelie would neuer haue returned) put them in such feare, that they wist not what to make of the matter, and so (as men amazed) they yéelded without anie further exception. The bishop of Durham bringing those The castel of Tickhill yéelded. *Rog. Houed.*prisoners with him which had yéelded vp this castell of Tickhill, came to the king the 27 daie of March, the verie daie before that Notingham castell was giuen ouer.

Strife betwixt y^earchbishops for carieng of their crosses.Moreouer, this is to be remembred, that during the siege of Notingham, contention arose betwixt the two archbishops of Canturburie and Yorke, about the carriage of their crosses. For Hubert archbishop of Canturburie comming thither, had his crosse borne before him; the archbishop of Yorke (hauing no crosse there at all) was verie sore offended, that anie other should go with crosse borne before him in his diocesse, and therfore complained [247]hereof to the king. But the archbishop of Canturburie mainteined that he had not doone anie thing but that which was lawfull for him to doo, and therevpon made his appeale to Rome, that the pope might haue the hearing and iudging of that controuersie betwixt them.

In the meane time, after the king had got the castells of Notingham and Tickhill into his hands (as ye haue heard) he called a parlement at Notingham, where the quéene mother sat on the right hand of him, and the archbishops of Canturburie & Yorke on the left, with other bishops, earles and barons according to their places. On the first daie of their Officers discharged.session was Gerard de Camuille discharged of the office which he had borne of shiriffe of Lincolne, and dispossessed both of the castell & countie. And so likewise was Hugh Bardolfe of the castell and countie of Yorke, and of the castell of Scarbourgh, and of the custodie and kéeping Lieutenantships set on sale.of the countrie of Westmerland, the which offices being now in the kings hands, he set them on sale to him that would giue most. Hereof it came to passe, that where the lord chancellour offered to giue fiftéene hundred markes before hand, for the counties of Yorke, Lincolne and Northampton, and an hundred markes of increase of rent for euerie of the The archbishop of Yorks offer.same counties, Geffrey archbishop of Yorke offered to the king thrée thousand markes aforehand, onelie for the countie of Yorke, and an hundred markes yearelie of increase, and so had the same committed to his regiment.

The bishop of Chester.Moreouer in this parlement, the king demanded iudgement against his brother John, and Hugh Nouant the bishop of Couentrie and Chester, for such traitorous and most disloiall attempts as they had made against him and his countries, and iudgement was giuen that both the said earle and bishop should haue summons giuen them peremptorilie to appeare, and if within fortie daies after, they came not to answer such plaints as might be laid against them, then should earle John forfeit all that he had within the realme, and the bishop should stand to the iudgement of the bishops, in that he was a bishop, and to the temporall lords in that he had béene the kings shiriffe.

A subsidie.In this parlement also, in the kalends of Aprill, the king procured a subsidie to be granted to him, to wit, two shillings of euerie plough land through England, which maner of subsidie by an old name is called Teemen toll, or Theyme toll. He also commanded that euerie man should make for him the third part of knights seruice, accordinglie as euerie fée might beare, to furnish him foorth into Normandie. He demanded of the moonks Cisteaux, all their wooles for the same yeare. But bicause that seemed an ouer greeuous burthen vnto them, they fined with him, as after shall appeare. The fourth day of this parlement, by the kings permission manie greeuous complaints were exhibited against the The archbishop of Yorke accused.archbishop of Yorke, for extortion and other vniust vexations, which he had practised: but he passed so little thereof, that he made no answer vnto their billes.

Gerard de Camuille charged with felonie and treason.Moreouer through the procurement of the lord chancellour, Gerard de Camuille was arreigned for receiuing théeues, and robbers, which had robbed certeine merchants of their goods, that were going to the faire of Stamfort; also they appealed him of treason for refusing to stand to his triall by order of the kings lawes at commandement of the kings iustices, bearing himselfe to be earle Johns man, and aiding the same earle against the king. But all these accusations he flatlie denied, and so his aduersaries put in pledges to follow their suit, and he put in the like to defend himselfe by one of his fréeholders.

The king of Scots commeth to sée the king of England.The same daie king Richard receiued the king of Scots at Clipstone, comming now to visit him, and to reioise with him for his safe returne home after so long a iournie, and so manie passed perils. After they had spent the time a certeine space in ioy and mirth, the fourth of Aprill at their being togither at Malton, the king of Scots required of king Richard to haue restored to him the counties of Northumberland, Cumberland and Westmerland, with the countie of Lancaster also, the which in right of his predecessors belonged to him (as he alledged.)

[248]A parlement.King Richard assembling a parlement of the Nobles of his realme at Northampton, about sixtéene daies after that the Scotish king had made this request, gaue him answer that by no means he might as then satisfie his petition: for if he should so doo, his aduersaries in France would report that he did it for feare, and not for any loue or hartie A grant made to the king of Scots what allowance he should haue when he came to England.fréendship. But yet king Richard in the presence of his mother quéene Elianor, and the lords spirituall and temporall of his realme togither at that present assembled, granted and by his déed confirmed vnto the said king of Scots, and to his heires for euer, that whensoeuer he or any of them should come by summons of the king of England vnto his court, the bishop of Durham, and the shiriffe of Northumberland should receiue him at the water of Twéed, and safe conduct him vnto the water of These, and there should the archbishop of Yorke, and the shiriffe of Yorke be readie to receiue him of them, and from thence giue their attendance vpon him vnto the borders of the next shire.

It was also granted to the said king, that he should be attended from shire to shire by prelats and shiriffes, till he came to the kings court, also from the time that the king of Scotland should enter this realme of England, he should haue dailie out of the kings pursse for his liuerie an hundred shillings, and after he came to the court, he should haue an allowance dailie for his liuerie, so long as he there remained, thirtie shillings and twelue manchet wastels, twelue manchet simnels, foure gallons of the best wine, and eight gallons of houshold wine, two pound of pepper, foure pound of cumin, two stone of wax, or else foure links, and fortie great and long colpons of such candels as are serued before the king, and foure and twentie colpons of other candels that serue for the houshold. And when he should returne into his countrie againe, then should he be conueied with the bishops and shiriffes from countie to countie, till he come to the water of Twéed, hauing an hundred shillings a day of liuerie, &c: as is before appointed. The charter of this grant was deliuered vnto William king of Scots in the towne of Northampton, in Easter wéeke, by the hands of William bishop of Elie lord chancellour, in the yeare of our lord 1194, and in the fift yeare of king Richard his reigne.

A councell holden at Winchester.After this, on the fiftéenth day of Aprill, king Richard hauing the said king of Scots in his companie came to Winchester, where he called a councell, and there in open assemblie he highlie commended all those of the Nobilitie, that in his absence had shewed themselues faithfull, and resisted his brother, and such other his complices, which had as disloiall persons rebelled against him. Here he also proclaimed his said brother, and all those that tooke his part, traitours to the crowne, and tooke order for the punishment of them, that (being of their faction) could by any means be apprehended.

Furthermore, to put awaie as it were the reproofe of his captiuitie and imprisonment (by the reuiuing of his noblenesse, which he had in high estimation.

—— pretio nam dignior omni estNobilitas, hæc non emitur nec venditur auro)

The king crowned anew.he caused himselfe to be eftsoones crowned by the archbishop Hubert, on the 18 of Aprill, at Winchester, and so shewed himselfe as a new crowned king (in hope of good successe and better lucke to follow) in the R. *Houed.* The king of Scots beareth one of the swords before the king of England.presence of the said king of Scots, who bare one of the thrée swords before him, going in the middle betwixt two earles, that is to saie, Hamelin earle of Warren going on his right hand, and Ranulfe earle of Chester on his left. The canapie vnder the which he went was borne vp also by foure earles,

Norffolke, Lislewight, Salisburie, and Ferrers. The bishop of Elie lord chancellour went on the right hand of the king, and the bishop of London on the left. At dinner also the citizens of The citizens of London.London serued him in the butterie by reason of two hundred marks which they had giuen the king that they might so doo, notwithstanding the claime and challenge made by the citizens of Winchester, the which serued him in the kitchin.

The archbishop of Yorke was commanded that he should not be present at the coronation, least some tumult might arise about the hauing of his crosse borne afore him, to [249]the displeasure of the archbishop of Canturburie, who stood in it, that no prelat within his prouince ought to haue any crosse borne before him, himselfe excepted.

A parlement called.After this, he called a parlement, by vertue whereof he reuoked backe and resumed into his hands all patents, annuities, fées, and other grants (before his voiage into the holie land) by him made, or otherwise granted or alienated. And bicause it shuld not seeme that he vsed a méere violent extortion herein, he treated with euerie one of them in most courteous wise, bearing them in hand, that he knew well they ment not to let foorth their monie to him vpon vsurie, but would be contented with such reasonable gaine and profit, as had béene raised to their vse in time of his absence of those things which they held of him by assignation in way of lone, so that now the same might be restored to him againe, sith he ment not to sell them, but to let them foorth as it were to farme for the time, as all men might well vnderstand, considering that he could not mainteine the port of a king without receipt of those profits which he had so let foorth. With these gentle The bold courage of the bishop of Lincolne.words therefore mixed with some dreadfull allegations, he brought them all into such perplexitie, that not one of them durst withstand his request, nor alledge that he had wrong doone to him, except Hugh the bishop of Lincolne, who sticked not to saie, that the king in this The bishop of Durham lost his earledome.demand did them and the rest open iniurie. The bishop of Durham lost his earledome, and was constreined to content himselfe with his old bishoprike, and to leaue the dignitie of an earle, or at the leastwise the possessions which he had bought of the king before his setting forward into the holie land.

Thus the king recouered those things for the which he had receiued great summes of monie, without making any recompense, where the most part of the occupiers had not receiued scarselie a third part of the principall which they had laid foorth. For no sufficiencie of grant, patent, or other writing to any of them before made, did any thing auaile them. K. Richards practises. The moonks Cisteaux.Moreouer, where he had borrowed a great summe of monie of the merchants of the staple, he wrought a feat with the moonks of the Cisteaux order to discharge that debt. He told these moonks that being constreined with vrgent necessitie, he had borowed that monie of the merchants beyond the sea, vpon confidence of their good beneuolence, and therefore he required them to extend their liberallitie so farre toward him, as to deliuer so much wooll in value, as should discharge that debt. To be short, the moonks being ouercome with the kings words, threatning kindnesse vpon them, fulfilled his request. Moreouer not satisfied herewith, he leuied a taske throughout the realme, exacting of euerie hide of land two shillings, according to the grant made to him at Notingham: and the same was generallie gathered, as well of the spirituall mens lands as of the temporall.

Rog. Houed. The king of Scots maketh suit for Northumberland.The king of Scots vnderstanding that the bishop of Durham had giuen ouer and resigned the earledome of Northumberland into the kings hands, thought good once againe to assaie if he might compasse his desire, and herewith he began his former suit afresh, offering to king Richard fiftéene thousand markes of siluer for the whole earledome of Northumberland with the appurtenances, as his father earle Henrie did hold the same before. The king taking counsell in the matter, agreed that he should haue it for that monie, excepting the castels: but the king of Scots would haue castels and all, or else he would not bargaine.

Finallie, after he had sundrie times mooued this suit for the hauing of the lands vnto which he pretended a title, and could get nothing of king Richard but faire words, putting him as it were in hope to obteine that he required at his next returne out of France, vpon the 22 daie of Aprill being fridaie, he tooke leaue of the king, and returned towards his countrie, not verie ioifull, in that he could not obteine his suit. King Richard in this meane while

44

caused all those prisoners that were taken in the castels of Notingham, Tickhill, Marleburgh, Lancaster[13], and Mainprise.S. Michaels mount, which were of any wealth to be put in prison, that they might fine for their ransoms. The residue he suffered to depart [250]vpon suerties, that were bound for them in an hundredth marks a peece, to be forth comming when they should be called.

Now the king (after he had gathered a great portion of monie, and ordeined diuerse things for the behoofe of the common-wealth, thereby to satisfie the harts of the people) prepared himselfe to saile into *Rog. Houed.*Normandie. But first he reconciled the archbishop of Yorke, and the bishop of Elie lord chancellour, aswell for the apprehension & imprisoning of the archbishop at Douer, as for the dishonourable expulsion of the chancellour out of England, in such wise that the chancellour should vpon reasonable summons giuen to him by the archbishop, sware with the hands of an hundred préests with him, that he neither commanded nor willed that the archbishop should be apprehended. The controuersie betwixt the two archbishops about the bearing of their crosses, the king would not meddle withall, for (as he said) that perteined to the pope. Yet the archbishop of Canturburie complained to king Richard of the iniurie doone to him at that present by the archbishop of Yorke, presuming within his prouince to haue his crosse borne before him. At length when the kings prouision was once readie for his voiage into Normandie, he came to Douer, and hearing that the French king had besieged the towne of Vernueil, and that the same was in danger to be taken, he tooke the sea togither with his mother quéene Elianor on The king transporteth ouer into France.the ninth daie of Maie, and transporting ouer into Normandie, arriued at Harfléet with an hundred great ships fraught with men, horsses and armour.

The French king hearing of king Richards arriuall, and that he was comming with a great power to the succour of them within Vernueil, and The French king raiseth his siege from Vernueil.was alreadie incamped néere to the towne of the Eagle, he plucked vp his tents in the night before Witsundaie, and leauing the siege, departed from thence, and tooke a certeine small fortresse by the waie as he marched, wherein he left a few souldiers to keepe it to his vse. King Richard herewith entring into the French dominions, sent three bands of souldiers towards Vale de Ruell, and went himselfe vnto Loches, and besieging that castell wan it within a short time. The Normans also *N. Triuet.*recouered the citie of Eureux out of the French mens hands, but those that were sent vnto Ruell, and had besieged the castell there an eight daies without any gaine, hearing that the French king was comming towards them, departed thence, & came backe to the kings campe, wherevpon the French king comming to Ruell raced it to the ground, bicause his enimie should not at anie time in winning it nestle there to the further damage of the countrie.

*Rog. Houed.*About the same time, Robert earle of Leicester issuing foorth of Rouen in hope to worke some feat to the damage of the Frenchmen, as he rode The earle of Leicester taken prisoner.somewhat vnaduisedlie in the lands of Hugh Gourney, fell within danger of his enimies, who tooke him prisoner, and a few other that were in his companie. The French king after this came with his armie into the coasts of Touraine; and marched neere Vandosme, and there incamped, whereof king Richard being aduertised, drew néere to Vandosme, meaning to assaile the French king in his campe, who hauing knowledge thereof dislodged with his armie earlie in the morning, and fled awaie (to his great dishonour) in all hast possible. The king of England with his people following in chase of the Frenchmen slue manie, and tooke a great number of prisoners, amongst whome was the French kings chéefe treasurer. Also the Englishmen tooke manie wagons and sumpters laden with crossebowes, armour, plate, apparell, and the furniture of the French kings chapell. This chanced about 37 daies after his fléeing in the night from Vernueil, of which two flights of the French king (in manner as ye haue heard) we find these verses written:

Gallia fugisti bis, & hoc sub rege Philippo,Nec sunt sub modio facta pudenda tuo.Vernolium sumit testem fuga prima, secundaVindocinum, noctem prima, secunda diem.[251]Nocte fugam primam rapuisti, manè secundam,Prima nictus vitio, víq; secunda fuit.

France, twice thou fledst, while Philip reign'd,the world dooth know thy shame,For Vernueil witnesse beares of th' one,next Vandosme knowes the same.The first by night, the next by day,thy heart and force doo showe,That first through feare, and next by force,was wrought thine ouerthrowe.

Geffrey de Rancon. The earle of Engolesme. The king of Nauars brother.In this meane while certeine rebels in Guien, as the lord Geffrey de Rancin[14] or Rancon, and the earle of Engolesme with their complices, vpon confidence of the French kings assistance, sore disquieted the countrie. Howbeit, the sonne of the king of Nauarre, and brother to Berengaria the quéene of England, entring into Guien with an armie, wasted the lands of both those rebels, till he was called home by reason of his fathers An. Reg. 6.death which chanced about the same time. Shortlie after Geffrey Rancin died, and king Richard comming into his countrie, wan the strong castell of Tailleburge by surrender, which apperteined to the same Geffrey with others, and then going against the other rebels, he wan the citie of Engolesme woone.Engolesme from him by force of assault. All which time the French king stirred not, by reason that there was some communication in hand for a truce to be taken betwixt him and king Richard, which by mediation of certeine bishops was shortlie after concluded, to endure for twelue monethes. The bishop of Elie was chéefe commissioner for the king of *Polydor. Wil. Paruus.*England, and this truce was accorded about Lammas, and serued to little purpose, except to giue libertie to either prince to breath a little, *Polydor.*and in the meane time to prouide themselues of men, munition, ships & monie, that immediatlie after the terme was expired, they might with greater force returne to the field againe, for they had not onelie a like desire to follow the warres, but also vsed a like meane and practise to leuie monie.

Great exactions.For whereas they had alreadie made the temporaltie bare with often paiments, and calling them foorth to serue personallie in the warres, they thought best now to fetch a fleece from the spiritualtie and churchmen, considering also that they had béene by reason of their immunitie more gentlie dealt with, and not appointed to serue themselues The colour pretended in leuieng of monie.in anie maner of wise. To colour this exaction which they knew would be euill taken of manie, they bruted abroad, that they leuied this monie vpon purpose, to send it into the holie land, towards the paiment of the christian souldiers, which remained there vpon defense of those townes, which yet the Saracens had not conquered. King Richard therfore comming to Towrs in Touraine, required a great summe of monie of the cleargie in those parts, and the like request he made throughout all those his dominions, on that further side of the sea. King Philip for his part demanded likewise intollerable tithes and duties of all the churchmen in his territories, and those that had the gathering of that monie serued their owne turne, in dealing most streightlie with sillie préests, making them to paie what they thought good, though sometime beyond the bounds of equitie and reason.

Rog. Houed. Inquisitions taken by a iurie of sundrie matters.In September, the iustices itinerants made their circuits thorough euerie shire and countie of this realme, causing inquisitions to be taken by substantiall iuries of plées of the crowne both old and new, of recognisances, of escheats, of wards, of mariages, of all maner of offendors against the lawes and ordinances of the relme, and of all other transgressors, falsifiers, and murtherers of Jewes; of the pledges, goods, lands, debts, and writings of Jewes that were slaine, and of other circumstances touching that matter. Likewise of the accompts of shiriffes, as to vnderstand what had béene giuen towards the [252]kings ransome, how much had béene receiued, and what remained behind to receiue. Also of the lands that belonged to erle John, and what goods he had, and what he held in demaine, in wards, escheats, and in gifts, and for what cause they were giuen. Furthermore, of his fautors and partakers, which had made fines with the king, and which not, with manie Vsurers.other articles touching the same earle. Also of vsurers, and of their goods being seized, of wines sold contrarie to the assise, of false measures, and of such as hauing receiued the crosse to go into the holie land, died before they set forward. Also of grand assises that were of an hundred shillings land or vnder, and of defaults, and of diuerse other things, the iurats were charged to inquire, and present the same.

The iustices also were appointed to cause the manours, farmes and lands which the king held in demaine, or by wards and escheats, to be suruéied by a substantiall iurie, and to take order for the conuerting of them to such vse, as the king might be answered of the gaines rising by the same Iewes.at the farmers hands. Also, the Iewes were appointed to inroll all their debts, pledges, lands, houses, rents and possessions. Moreouer, Iustices, shiriffes and other officers.inquisition was taken of iustices, shiriffes, bailiffes, conestables, foresters and other officers belonging to the king, to vnderstand in what maner they had behaued themselues in taking and seizing of things into their hands, and of all such goods, gifts and promises had and receiued by occasion of leasure made of the lands of earle John and his fautors, and who receiued the same, and what delaie was granted by Hubert archbishop of Canturburie lord chéefe iustice.commandement of Hubert archbishop of Canturburie, then lord chéefe iustice.

In this meane time, whilest these inquisitions were thus taken in England, king Richard comming foorth of Poictou into Aniou, caused all the bailiffes and officers of that countrie, and also of Maine, to fine Officers driuen to fine for their offices. The king offended with the lord chauncellor.with him for their offices. After this, when he came downe into Normandie, he séemed in shew to be offended with his chancellour the bishop of Elie, about concluding of the truce with the French king (where as ye haue heard he was cheefe commissioner) misliking greatlie all that was doone therein, and therefore he tooke the seale from him, and caused a new seale to be made, commanding to be proclaimed thorough all his dominions, that whatsoeuer had béene sealed with the old seale, should stand in no force, both for that his chancellor had wrought more vndiscreetlie than was conuenient; and againe, bicause the same seale A new seale.was lost, when Roger Malus Catulus his vicechancellour was drowned, who perished, among other by shipracke, néere to the Ile of Cypres, before the king arriued there, being as then on his iournie into the holie land. Therefore all men had commandement to come to this new seale, that they might haue their charters and writings confirmed.

Matth. Paris. The king returneth into England. He granteth the English men licence to tournie.Furthermore, whilest the truce yet lasted, king Richard sailed ouer into England, where he caused turnies to be exercised in diuerse places, for the better training vp of souldiers in feats of warre, that they might growe more skilfull and perfect in the same, when they should come to the triall of their forces, whereby he raised no small summes of monie for granting license to his subiects so to tournie. Euerie earle that would tournie, paid to him for his licence twentie marks, euerie baron *Rog. Houed.* Fines paid for licence to exercise turnements.ten marks, and euerie knight hauing lands, did giue foure marks, and those that had no lands two marks, to the great damnifieng of the people; hauing learned the common lesson, and receiued the ordinarie rule followed of all, and neglected of none; namelie,

Mal. Pal. in suo sap.——— opus est nummis vel morte relictis,Vel sorte inuentis, vel quauis arte paratis,Quippe inopem mala multa pati contingit vbíq;,Nec sine diuitijs fas cuiquam ducere vitamFœlicem, &c.

The charter of this grant was deliuered by the king vnto William earle of Salisburie, to haue the kéeping thereof: but Hubert Walter the archbishop of Canturburie, and lord [253]chéefe iustice, bade his brother Theobald Walter collector of the monie, for the scraping and raking togither whereof, in huge sums, he put the former shifts of extortion and exaction in practise.

The tenour of the charter concerning the turnements before remembred.

Richard by the grace of God king of England, duke of Normandie and Aquitaine, and earle of Aniou, to the reuerend father in Christ, Hubert archbishop of Canturburie, and primat of all England, sendeth greeting. Know ye that we haue granted turnaments to be kept in England in fiue steeds, to wit, betwixt Sarisburie and Wilton, betwixt Warwike and Kenelworth, betwixt Stanford and Warmeford, betwixt Brackley and Nixburgh, betwixt Blie & Tickhill, so that the peace of our land be not broken, nor yet our iustices authoritie diminished, nor any damage doone to our forrests. Prouided that what earle soeuer will turney there, shall giue to vs twentie markes, a baron ten marks, a knight that hath lands foure marks and he that hath no lands shall giue two marks.

Moreouer, no stranger shall be admitted to turney there, wherevpon we command you, that at the daie of the turnieng, ye haue there two clarkes, and two of our knights to receiue the oth of the earles and barons, which shall satisfie vs of the said summes of monie, before the turnieng begin, and that they suffer none to turnie, till (before) they haue made paiment, and haue caused to be entred how much & of whom they haue receiued: and ye shall take ten marks for this charter to our vse, whereof the earle of Salisburie, and the earle of Clare, and the earle Bishops towne.of Warren are pledges. Witnesse myselfe, at Ville Leuesche, the two and twentith of August.

Furthermore, ordinances were made and set foorth for the safe keeping of the peace, so that such as would turney, neither by the waie in comming or going, or whilest the turnieng lasted, should violentlie take any thing to serue their necessarie vses, without paieng therefore to the owner according to the woorth, nor should doo iniurie to any man in any manner of wise. But now to the other dooings of king Richard, who made I thinke he came not ouer at all into England at this time, but rather sent his mind vnto the archbishop.no long abode in England at this time, but shortlie returned into Normandie, bicause he heard that king Philip had an armie readie leuied. Wherefore meaning to buckle with him vpon occasion offered, he made the more hast, and being landed there, approched vnto the borders of the French dominions, incamping himselfe with his armie in the field, to wait for the time that the truce should be expired, least the enimie should in any exploit preuent him. In like manner king Philip hauing with him earle John king Richards brother, kept his souldiers and men of warre in a readines with him, to worke any feat that should be thought expedient assoone as the truce should end.

1195.Whilest both these kings were thus bent to powre out their malice, and to ease their stomachs with dint of sword, there came messengers from Messengers from the pope, exhorting him vnto peace and quietnesse, but his exhortation little auailed.pope.the For they regarding it little or nothing, immediatlie as the truce was expired, got them abroad into the field, & king Richard Isoldune.drew towards Isoldune, a towne situat in the confines of Berrie, whither it was reported that the French king meant to come: and there staid for him a whole day togither. But the French king hearing that king Richard was there to looke for him, thought it best not to come there at all. Wherefore king Richard went the next daie vnto a castell called Brison, and tooke it vpon his first approch. Then went he to a towne called Nouencourt and perceiuing the same to be strong and well manned, tooke not in hand to assaile it till the third daie after his comming thither, at what time he so [254]inclosed the same round about with diligent watch and ward, that a cat could not haue escaped out of the place, neither by Nouencourt yéeldeth to K. Richard. Albermarle besieged. *Matt. West.Polydor.*daie nor night, but that she should haue béene espied. They within being put in feare herewith, yeelded vp the towne the daie next following, in which meane time the French king besieged Albemarle.

Herevpon king Richard, hauing left a garrison of souldiers in Nouencourt, came to raise the enimie from his siege, & setting vpon the Frenchmen, there began a sharpe fight: but the Englishmen being wearie with trauell of their passed iournie, and hauing rashlie entred into the battell, were not able to indure the Frenchmens violence, so that (not without great losse) they were constreined to retire with swift flight, or (to saie the truth) to run awaie a maine pase. The French king hauing thus chased his enimies, returned to assault Albemarle, woone the castell by force, and the towne by composition, permitting the garrison there to depart with all their armour. This doone, he ruinated the *Rog. Houed.* The earle of Leicesters offer for his ransome.castell flat to the ground. Robert earle of Leicester offered to the French king a thousand marks sterling for his ransome, and to quite claime to him and his heires for euer all the right which he had to the castell of Pascie, with the appurtenances, and to get a confirmation thereof for him both of the pope, and of the king of England: but for that the warre still lasted, the French king tooke a respite in answering this offer, neuerthelesse afterwards in the yeare next insuing, he tooke it, and so the earle was set at libertie.

Not long after this foresaid repulse, the king of England hauing refreshed his souldiers with some rest after their great trauell, went Million won and rased.to Million, and giuing assault to the towne wan it at the first brunt, and made it plaine with the earth. Then was a motion made for peace A motion for peace.betwixt the two kings, being now wearied with long wars: whereof when earle John was aduertised, who (as it should séeme by some writers) hauing tarried with the French king till this present, began now to doubt least if any agréement were made, he might happilie be betraied of the French king by couenants that

48

should passe betwixt them: he determined therefore with himselfe to commit his whole safetie to his naturall brother, and to no man else, perceiuing that the French king made not so great accompt of him after the losse of his castels in England, as he had doone before.

Herevpon comming to his brother king Richard, "he besought him to pardon his offense, and though he had not dealt brotherlie towards him, yet that he would brotherlie forgiue him his rebellious trespasse, adding furthermore, that whereas he had not heretofore beene thankefull for his manifold benefits which he had receiued at his hands, yet he was now most sorie therefore, and was willing to make amends: wherewith he acknowledged the safegard of his life to rest in him, for the which he was bound to giue him thanks, if he would grant thereto." The king mooued with his words, made this answer (as it is said) that he pardoned him indéed, but yet wished that he might forget such iniuries as he had receiued at his hands, which he doubted least he should not easilie doo. Earle John returneth to the king his brother, and is pardoned. Herewith erle John being yet put in good hope of forgiuenesse, sware to be true euer after vnto him, and that he would endeuour himselfe to make amends for his misdeeds past, and so was shortlie after restored vnto his former degree, honour and estimation *Wil. Paruus. R. Houed.Matth. Paris.* in all respects.

But by some writers it should appeare, that earle John, immediatlie vpon conclusion of the first truce, came from the French king, and submitted himselfe to his brother, and by mediation of the quéene their mother was pardoned, receiued againe into fauour, and serued euer after against the *Rog. Houed.* French king verie dutifullie, séeking by new atchiued enterprises brought about (to the contentation of his brother) to make a recompense for his former misdemeanor, reputing it meere madnesse to make means to further mischeefe; for

—— stultum est hostem iritare potentem,Atq; malum maius tumidis sibi quærere verbis.

R. Houed. But at what time soeuer he returned thus to his brother, this yeare (as Roger Houeden [255]saith) he was restored to the earledoms of Mortaigne in Normandie, and Glocester in England, with the honour of Eie (the castels onelie excepted) and in recompense of the residue of the earledoms which he had before inioied, togither with certeine other lands, his brother king Richard gaue vnto him a yeerelie pension amounting to the summe of *Rog. Houed. Wil. Paruus.Matth. Paris. Polychron.* eight thousand pound of Aniouin monie. ¶ Now here to staie a while at matters chancing here about home, I will speake somewhat of the dooings of Leopold duke of Austrich, who as one nothing mooued with the pestilence and famine that oppressed his countrie in this season, but rather hauing his hart hardened, began to threaten the English hostages that they shuld loose their liues, if king Richard kept not the couenants which he had vndertaken to performe by a day appointed. Baldwin de Betun.Wherevpon Baldwin Betun one of the hostages was sent by common agréement of the residue vnto king Richard, to signifie to him their estate. King Richard willing to deliuer them out of further danger, sent with the same Baldwin his coosen, the sister of Arthur duke of Britaine, and the daughter of the emperour of Cypres, to be conueied vnto the said duke of Austrich, the one, namelie the sister of Arthur to be ioined in marriage with the dukes sonne, and the other to continue in the dukes hands to bestow at his pleasure.

Duke Leopold catcheth a fall beside his horsse and dieth of the hurt.But in the meane time, on saint Stephans day, duke Leopold chanced to haue a fall beside his horsse, and hurt his leg in such wise, that all the surgions in the countrie could not helpe him, wherevpon in extreame anguish he ended his life. And whereas before his death he required to be absolued of the sentence of excommunication pronounced against him by the pope (for apprehending of king Richard in his returning from his iournie made into the holie land) he was answered by the cleargie, that except he would receiue an oth to stand to the iudgement of the church for the iniurie doone to king Richard, and that vnlesse other of the Nobilitie would receiue the like oth with him if he chanced to die (whereby he might not fulfill that which the church héerein should decrée) that yet they should see the same performed, he might not otherwise be absolued.

Wherefore he tooke the oth, and the Nobles of his countrie with him, and therewithall released the English pledges, remitted the monie that yet remained behind of his portion aforesaid, and immediatlie therewith died. After his deceasse, bicause certeine péeres of the countrie withstood the performance of the premisses, his bodie laie eight daies longer aboue ground than otherwise it should haue doone, for till such time as all the pledges were perfectlie released, it might not be buried. Also Baldwin de Betun approching neere to the confines of Austrich, when he heard that the duke was dead, returned with the two ladies vnto his souereigne lord king Richard. Thus (as ye haue heard) for feare of the censures of the church were the pledges restored, and the residue of the monie behind released.

¶ All this was both pleasant and profitable for king Richards soules helth (as may be thought) bicause he tooke occasion therof to amend his owne former life, by considering how much he might be reprehended for his sundrie faults committed both against God and man. A maruellous matter to heare, how much frō that time forward he reformed his former trade of liuing into a better forme & order. Moreouer, the White moonks.emperour gaue to the Cisteaux moonks 3000 marks of siluer, parcell of king Richards ransome, to make siluer censers in euerie church throughout where they had any houses: but the abbats of the same order refused the gift, being a portion of so wrongfull and vngodlie a gaine. At which thing, when it came to the knowledge of K. Richard, he greatlie maruelled at the first, but after commended the abbats in their dooings, and cheeflie for shewing that they were void of the accustomed gréedinesse of hauing, which most men supposed them to be much infected withall.

Rog. Houed. Hugh Nouāt bishop of Couentrie restored to his sée. The archbishop of Yorke.King Richard this yeare pardoned Hugh Nouant bishop of Couentrie of all his wrath and displeasure conceiued toward him, and restored to him his bishoprike for fiue thousand marks of siluer. But Robert Nouant the same bishops brother died in the kings prison at Douer. Also whereas the archbishop of Yorke had offended king Richard, he [256]pardoned him, and receiued him againe into fauour, with the kisse of peace. Wherevpon the archbishop waxed so proud, that vsing the king reprochfullie, he lost his archbishoprike, the rule of Yorkeshire which he had in gouernment as shiriffe, the fauour of his souereigne, and (which was the greatest losse of all) the loue of God. For

*M. Pal. in suo sag.*Nemo superbus amat superos, nec amator ab illis,Vult humiles Deus ac mites, habitatq; libenterMansuetos animos procul ambitione remotos,Inflatos verò ac ventosos deprimit idem,Nec patitur secum puro consistere olympo.

Pope Celestine. The archbish. of Canturburie is made ye popes legat.Moreouer, through the kings request, pope Celestine this yeare made the archbishop of Canturburie legat of all England by his buls directed to him, bearing date at his palace in Rome called Lateran the fifteenth kalends of Aprill, in the fourth yeare of his papasie. Furthermore, the pope wrote to the English cleargie, giuing them to vnderstand that he had created the said archbishop of Canturburie his legat, commanding them so to accept him: by vertue of which letters, the archbishop Hubert A trinitie of officers in vnitie of person.being now both archbishop of Canturburie, legat of the apostolike sée, and lord chéefe iustice of England, appointed to hold a councell at Yorke, and therefore gaue knowledge by the abbat of Binham in Northfolke, and one maister Geruise, vnto the canons of Yorke, and to the archbishops officials of his purposed intention.

The said canons and officials well considering of the popes letters, which were deliuered vnto them by the messengers, signified for answer, that they would gladlie receiue him as legat of the apostolike sée, but not as archbishop of Canturburie, nor as their primat. Herewith he came to Yorke vpon saint Barnabies daie being sundaie, and was receiued with procession. On the morrow after, he held a court of plees of the crowne, of assises, and such other matters touching the king. On the next day being Tuesday, he entred into the monasterie of saint Maries in Yorke, and deposed the abbat, bicause of his infirmitie of bodie, at the request of the moonks, but the abbat appealed to the popes consistorie. A synod holden at Yorke.Then he assembled the cleargie in the church of Saint Peter in Yorke, and there held a synod for reformation of things amisse in the church, and amendment of manners in the cleargie, so that diuerse decrées were made, the which for bréefenesse we omit to speake of in particular. This yeare also, the said archbishop Hubert caused all men throughout the realme of England to receiue an oth of obseruing the kings peace, and to sweare that they should not be robbers, nor abbettors of robbers, nor in any wise consenting vnto them, but should doo what in them might lie to apprehend all such offendors, and to discouer them to the kings officers to be apprehended, and to pursue them vpon hew and crie to the vttermost of their powers, and those that withdrew themselues from such pursuit, should be apprehended as partakers with the offendors.

The emperor sendeth to the king.About this time the emperour sent to king Richard, requiring him in no wise to conclude any peace with the French king, but rather to inuade An. Reg. 7.his dominions, promising to aid him all that he might. But king Richard, to vnderstand further of the emperours mind herein, sent ouer his The bishop of Elie is sent to the emperour.chancellour the bishop of Elie vnto him in ambassage. In the meane time the warre was still continued betwixt him and the French, by the which they were commonlie put to the worse, and king Richard inuading their borders, did much hurt in wasting the countries on each side. The French king was at one time so narrowlie chased, that as he would haue passed a bridge that laie ouer the water of Saine, he was in danger of drowning by the fall of the same vnder him, but yet at the length he escaped, and got to the further side.

The 2 kings talke togither.After this, the two kings came to a communication togither, in the which a motion was made, that Lewes the French king his sonne and heire should haue the sister of Arthur duke of Britaine in marriage, and that king Richard in consideration thereof should surrender vnto them and to their heires the townes of Gisors, Bademont, with the countrie of Veulquessine or Veuxine le Normant, Vernon, Iuerie and Pascie; and further should [257]giue vnto them twentie thousand marks of siluer. On the other side it was mooued, that the French king should resigne vnto king Richard all that he could demand in the countie of Engeulesme, and should restore vnto him the counties of Albemarle and Augie, with the castell of Arkes, and all other castels which he had taken in Normandie, or in any partie during these last warres. But there was a respit taken for the full concluding and assuring of these conditions, till the octaues of All saints, that king Richard might vnderstand the emperours pleasure, without whose consent he might not conclude any thing concerning that matter, bicause he had sent such word vnto him by the lord chancellour, who at this time was attendant in his court.

In the meane time, the emperour being aduertised of the whole matter, and of the articles afore mentioned, gaue knowledge to king Richard by the bishop of Elie at his returning backe, that this forme of peace nothing liked him, but rather made directlie to his discontentment: the which least he might séeme to saie without sufficient ground of reason, he alledged, that it should sound to king Richards dishonour, if he surrendred and gaue vp anie thing that he had not in possession. And to The emperor dissuadeth the king from agréeing to the peace.encourage him to recouer those things which had béene taken from him, the emperour pardoned him of the seauentéene thousand marks of siluer, which yet remained behind due to him for the kings ransome. Howsoeuer the matter passed, the two kings met not in the octaues of All saints, according to the appointment, although they were come, and approched verie néere to the place where they should haue communed togither: but through the dissimulation of the Frenchmen, they departed, without seeing one an other, and immediatlie began the warre as fiercelie as at anie time before.

The warre is begun afresh.The French king tooke the towne of Diep, which king Richard had latelie repared, and burned it, with the ships that harbored in the hauen: after this, commming to Isoldun, he wan the towne and besieged the castell. The hast which king Richard made.But king Richard aduertised thereof, came with quicke spéed (making of thrée daies iournie but one) and entred into the castell of Isoldun to defend the same against his aduersaries: and foorthwith there resorted such numbers of men vnto him, when they heard how he was besieged, that the French king doubting how to retire from thence in safetie, made suit first to haue licence to depart, and after when that would not be granted, he required at the leastwise to talke with the king of England about some agréement.

The 2 kings againe talke togither of peace.Wherevnto king Richard condescended, and so comming togither, they concluded vpon a truce to indure from that daie, being saturdaie next after the feast of saint Nicholas, vnto the feast of saint Hilarie next insuing, and then to méet againe néere vnto Louiers with their councels, that they might grow by some reasonable way vnto a finall peace and concord. And according to this article, shortlie after the same feast of 1196.S. Hilarie, they met at Louiers, where finallie they were accorded to conclude a peace on these conditions, that the French king should The conditions of peace concluded betwixt the two kings. *Matth. Paris.Matth. West.*release to the king of England Isoldun, with the countrie about, woon by him sith the beginning of these wars; likewise, all the right which he had in Berrie, Auuergine, and Gascoigne, and the countie of Albemarle. On the other part, the king of England should resigne Gisors, and certeine other places, and namelie Veuxine or Veulquesine vnto the king of France.

*Matth. West. Matth. Paris.*Herevpon were suerties also bound for performance, and the forfeiture of fiftéene thousand marks assigned to be paid by the partie that first brake the peace. Shortlie after, the French king repenting him selfe of the agreement, began to make a warre anew, so that king Richard seized into his hands all the goods and[15] possessions which belonged to the abbats of the order of the great monasterie of Clunie, and of saint Denise & la Charitie, which had become suertie for the French king in *Rog. Houed.* The earle of Albemarle departed this life.the summe of 1500 marks aforesaid. This yeare died William de Forz earle of Albemarle, in whose place succéeded Baldwine de Betun by the kings gift, and married the countesse of Albermarle.

Otho sonne to the duke of Saxonie.There was a motion also made for a marriage betwixt the lord Otho, sonne to Henrie duke of Saxonie, king Richards nephue by his sister, and the ladie Margaret, daughter to [258]the king of Scots, on as they should haue inioied the countries of Lothian, Northumberland, and the countie of Lawnes.Caerleill with the castels. For the conclusion of which marriage, the archbishop of Canturburie was sent about Christmas to commune with the king of Scots: but bicause the Scotish quéene was then conceiued of child, hir husband (in hope that God would send him a sonne) refused to stand vnto the aboue mentioned couenants.

*Wil. Paruus. Ran. Higd.*The abbat of Caen sent into England.At this time king Richard sent the abbat of Caen (who was also the elect of Durham) into England, to take an accompts of those that had the receipts of the kings monie: for this abbat had informed the king, that his receiuers and officers here in the realme dealt not iustlie in making their accompts, but both deceiued the king, and oppressed his people, in exacting more than was due, Fraudulent dealing in officers.and concealing that which they ought to stand accomptable for. The king supposing his words to be true, or at least likelie so to be, and that in reforming such vntruth in his officers, it should be both profitable to him, and well liked of the people, sent this abbat ouer with commission, to be as it were his generall auditour.

Howbeit, Hubert archbishop of Canturburie, which was gouernour of the realme in causes both temporall and spirituall (by reason he had the kings authorise as his vicegerent, & therefore sufficientlie countenanced, & also the popes as his legat authorised) did somewhat stomach the matter, in that it should be thought he did suffer such abuses in the kings officers, and not reforme them. But he held him content and said little, sith the abbat shewed him the kings commission to doo that which he went about, although he brought it not to passe. For whereas he came ouer in lent, and gaue out commandements, that all such as had any thing to doo in receipt of the kings monie, should appeare before him after Easter, he tarried not to see Easter himselfe, but was called into another world by the stroke of death, there to render accompts for his owne acts here in this life committed.

*Fabian. Wil. Paruus.Matt. Paris. Ran. Higd.*William Fitz Osbert.At the same time there was another person in London called William with the long beard, (aliàs Fitz Osbert) which had likewise informed the king of certeine great oppressions and excessiue outrages vsed by rich men against the poore (namelie the worshipfull of the citie, the Maior and Aldermen) who in their hoistings, when any tallage was to be gathered, The foule disorder in the citizens of London.burdened the poore further than was thought reason, to ease themselues; wherevpon[16] the said William being a seditious person, and of a busie nature, ceassed not to make complaints. Now bicause the king gaue eare vnto him at the first, he tooke a boldnesse thereof, & drawing vnto him great routs of the poorer sort of people, would take vpon him to defend the causes of those that found themselues greeued with the heauie yoke of richmen and gentlemen. He was somewhat learned, and verie eloquent: he had also a verie good wit, but he applied it rather to set dissention betwixt the high estates and the low, than to anie other good purpose. He accused also his owne brother of treason, who in his youth had kept *The vnnaturall ingratitude of Fitz Osbert.*him to schoole, & beene verie good and beneficiall brother vnto him, bicause now he would not still mainteine him with monie to beare out his riottous port. Moreouer, he declared to the king, that by extortion and briberie of certeine men of great wealth, he lost manie forfeits and escheats.

Manie gentlemen of honour sore hated him for his presumptuous attempts to the hindering of their purposes: but he had such comfort of the king, that he little passed for their malice, but kept on his intent, till the king being aduertised of the assemblies which he made, commanded him to ceasse from such dooings, that the people might fall againe to their sciences and occupations, which they had for the more part left off, at the instigation of this William with the long beard, so named of *Why he ware his long* berd.*Matth. Paris.*long heare of his beard, which he nourished of purpose to seeme the more graue and manlike, and also as it were in despite of them which counterfeited the Normans (that were for the most part shauen) and bicause he would resemble the ancient vsage of the English nation. The *Fabian.*kings commandement in restraint of the peoples resort vnto him, was well kept a while, but it was not long yer they began to follow him againe as they had doone before.

[259]Then he tooke vpon him to make vnto them certeine collations or sermons, taking for his theme, Haurietis aquas in gaudio de fontibus saluatoris, *His oration to the people.*that is to saie: Ye shall draw in gladnesse waters out of the founteins of your sauiour. And hereto he added, "I am (said he) the sauiour of poore men; ye be the poore, and haue assaied the hard hands and heauie burdens of the rich: now draw ye therefore the healthfull waters of vnderstanding out of my wels and springs, and that with ioy. For the time of your visitation is come: I shall part waters from waters, by waters I vnderstand the people, and I shall part the people which are good and méeke, from the people that are wicked and proud, and I shall disseuer the good and euill, euen as light is diuided from darknesse."

*Ger. Dor.*By these and such persuasions and means as he vsed, he had gotten two and fiftie thousand persons, readie to haue taken his part, as appeared after by a roll of their names found in his kéeping, besides diuerse instruments of iron to breake vp houses, and other things seruing to such like purposes. So that he brought the commoners into a great liking of him: but the rich and wealthie citizens stood in much feare, so that they kept their houses, in armes, in doubt to be robbed and murthred by him in the night season.

The archbishop of Canturburie (vnto whome the rule of the realme chéefelie belonged) being aduertised hereof, sent for the greatest number of the citizens, and vsing them with gentle words, persuaded them to deliuer pledges, the better to assure him, that no such thing should chance, which was suspected of manie, though he was loth to conceiue any such opinion of them. They being ouercome with his courteous words, gaue vnto him pledges.

*He is called before the archbishop of Canturburie lord chéefe iustice or president of the realme.*After this, when the foresaid William ceased not to make congregations of the people, at length the archbishop sent a commandement vnto him, that he should appeare before him and other of the councell, at a certeine prefixed daie, to answer to such things as might be laid to his charge. To be short, he did so at the time appointed, but with such a rout of the common people about him, that the archbishop durst not pronounce against him, but licenced him to depart for that time, giuing him soft and gentle words. Howbeit, certeine persons were then appointed by the said archbishop and other of the councell to watch him sometime, when he should haue no great companie about him, and then to apprehend him.

Amongst those that were thus commanded to attach him, were two burgesses of the citie, who hauing espied a conuenient time for the execution of their purpose, set vpon him to haue take him, but he getting an ax, defended himselfe manfullie: and in resisting slue one of them, and *He fléeth into the church of S. Marie Bow.*after that fled into the church of S. Marie Bow, kéeping the same not as a place of sanctuarie, but as a fortresse: in somuch that by the help of such as resorted vnto him, he defended it against his aduersaries, till with fire and smoke they constreined him to come foorth, and all those *His concubine.*that were there with him: amongst them also was his concubine, who neuer left him for any danger that might betide him.

The people regarding the danger of their pledges, came not out to aid him, as it was much doubted they would haue doone. Wherefore being thus attached, he was brought foorth, and comming out of the church, the sonne of that burgesse whome he had slaine (as you haue heard) strake him verie sore into the bellie with a knife, in reuenge of his fathers death. After this, he was had to his arraignment before the archbishop, sitting within the towre, and being condemned, was from thence drawne with horsses to the place of execution called the Elmes, and there He is executed. *Wil. Paruus. Matth. Paris.*hanged on a gibet, with nine of his adherents, which had defended the church against the kings power: and yet for all this, the grudge ceassed not, but the common people raised a great slander vpon the archbishop, both for causing him to be taken out of the church, where he claimed The archbishop of Canturburie is euill spokē of for ye death of William Fitz Osbert.priuilege of sanctuarie, and also for putting him to death, who was innocent (as they alledged) and not giltie of those crimes that were laid against him: who sought onelie the defense of poore people against extortioners, and such as were wrong dooers.

[260]This rumor rose so fast, that at length (by bruting abroad, that certeine miracles should be wrought by a chaine, wherein he was bound in An old whormonger, and a new saint.time of his imprisonment) he was taken for a saint. The place also where he suffered, was visited by women, and other superstitious folks, as a plot of great holinesse, till at length the archbishop caused it to be watched, to the end that no such foolishnesse should be vsed there. In fine, the opinion which the people had thus fondlie conceiued of his vertue and innocencie, was by little and little remooued out of their heads, when his acts were more certeinelie published: as the sleaing of a man with his owne hands, and the vsing of his concubine within Bowe church, during the time of his being there. Also the archbishop accursed a préest, which had first brought vp the false report and fained fable of the miracle wrought by the chaine, whereby the occasion of idolatrie was first giuen, and might easilie haue béene continued, if the archbishop had not béene the wiser man, and by such means repressed the rumour. ¶ So that we are to note by this example the force of counterfeit holinesse and feigned harmelesnesse in hypocrits,

——— qui pelle sub agniVipereum celant virus morésq; luporum;Et stolidos ficta virtutis imagine fallunt.

But now to return vnto the dooings of king Richard in France. Ye haue heard how a peace was concluded (as some haue written) but the same continued not long: for the French king séeming to repent himselfe of that he had doone (as is aforesaid) brake the peace, and raising a power, besieged Albemarle; at length wan it, and raced it downe to the ground, then king Richard gaue vnto him thrée thousand marks of siluer for the ransome of his knights and yeomen, or demilances (as I may call them) that were taken in that fortresse. After this, the French king wan Nouencourt, and earle Iohn tooke the castell of Gamages.

The erledome of Poictou.About the same time also king Richard gaue vnto his nephue Otho the earledome of Poictou. Which I haue thought good to note out of Roger Houeden, to remooue the doubt of Iohn Bouchet, John Bouchet his dout.who in the third part of his annales of Aquitaine, maruelleth at an old panchart or record which he had séene, by the tenour whereof it appeared, that this Otho intituled himselfe duke of Aquitaine and earle of Poictou, being in his castell of Monstereulbonin neere to Poictiers, in the yeare a thousand, one hundreth, ninetie nine, in presence of Geffrey de Lusignen, and others, and granted vnto a certeine person the office of cutting the monie in the mint of that towne, as by the same panchart it further appeareth.

The sight whereof brought the said Bouchet into a great perplexitie, considering that no chronicle which he had either seene, or heard of, made mention of any Otho that shuld be duke of Aquitaine, or erle of Poictou, either before that time, or after. Where againe it was euident to him, that queene Elianor the mother of king Richard, as then liuing, named hir selfe dutchesse of Aquitaine, and countesse of Poictou; & likewise king Richard intituled himselfe duke of Aquitaine, and earle of Poictou, euer after he had fianced the earle of

Barcelons daughter, as by diuerse records both of the mother and the sonne he had séene perfect notice. At length yet he gesseth (and that trulie) that it should be this Otho, to whom the mother and sonne had assigned the dutchie of Aquitaine and countie of Poictou, for the maintenance of his estate, he holding the same till the yeare 1199, in the which he was made emperour by king Richards good helpe, as after shall be shewed more at large.

Ranulph erle of Chester tooke his wife the dutchesse of Britaine prisoner. About this time also as the countesse of Britaine, the mother of duke Arthur came into Normandie to haue spoken with king Richard, Ranulph earle of Chester hir husband meeting hir at Pountourson, tooke hir as prisoner, and shut hir vp within his castell at S. James de Beumeron: and when hir sonne Arthur could not find means to deliuer hir out of captiuitie, he ioined with the king of France, and made great hauocke in the lands [261]of his vncle king Richard, whereupon the king gathered a mightie armie, and inuading Britaine with great force, cruellie wasted and destroied the countrie.

A dearth.Here is also to be noted, that in this seuenth yeare of king Richard, a great dearth chanced through this realme of England, and in the coasts about the same. Also about the same time died William earle of The death of the earle of Salisburie.Salisburie, the sonne of earle Patrike, whose daughter and heire king Richard gaue in marriage, togither with the earledome of Salisburie, vnto his base brother, surnamed Long Espée.

R. Houed. Matth. Paris.It chanced moreouer about the same time, that earle John the kings brother, with certeine capteins of such hired souldiors as some call Brabanceni; others, the Routs; and the French histories name them Costereaux, or Coterels, went abroad to atchiue some enterprise against the bishop of Beauuois, and other Frenchmen, which had doone much hurt to king Richards subiects in those parties. The chéefe leaders of those Routs or Costereaux, which went foorth with earle John, and serued vnder Marchades & Lupescaro.him at that time, were two Prouancois, Marchades & Lupescaro. These riding foorth into the countrie about Beauuois made hauocke in robbing and spoiling all afore them.

Anon as Philip the bishop of Beauuois, a man more giuen to the campe than to the church, had knowledge hereof, thinking them to be a méet preie for him, with sir William de Merlow and his sonne, and a great number of other valiant men of warre, came foorth into the fields, and encountring with the enimies, fought verie stoutlie. But yet in the end The bishop of Beauuois taken prisoner.the bishop, the archdeacon, and all the chéefe capteins were taken: the residue slaine and chased. After this, earle John and the foresaid capteins passed foorth, and wan the towne of Millie, and so returned.

Earle John and Marchades presented the two prelats with great triumph vnto K. Richard earlie in the morning, lieng yet in his bed; as those that were knowne to be his great enimies, saieng to him in French; "Rise Richard, rise, we haue gotten the great chantour of Beauuois, and a good quier man (as we take it) to answer him in the same note, and here we deliuer them vnto you to vse at your discretion." The king séeing them, smiled, and was verie glad for the taking of this bishop, for that he had euer found him his great aduersarie: and therefore being thus taken fighting in the field with armour on his backe, thought he might be bold in temporall wise to chastise him: sith he (not regarding his calling) practised to molest him with temporall weapons: whereupon he committed him to close prison all armed as he was.

It chanced soone after, that two of his chaplins came vnto the king to Rouen, where this bishop was deteined, beseeching the king of licence to attend vpon their maister now in captiuitie: vnto whome (as it is of some reported) the king made this answer; "I am content to make you iudges in the cause betwixt me and your maister, as for the euils which he hath either doone, either else gone about to doo vnto me, let the same be forgotten. This is true, that I being taken as I returned from my iournie made into the holie land, and deliuered into the emperours hands, was in respect of my kinglie state, vsed according thereunto verie fréendlie and honourablie, till your maister comming thither (for what purpose he himselfe best knoweth) had long conference with the emperour. After which, I for my part in the next morning tasted the fruit of their ouernights talke, being then loden with as manie irons as a good asse might not verie easilie haue borne. Iudge you therefore, what maner of imprisonment your maister deserued at my hands, that procured such ease for me at the emperours hands."

The two chaplins had their mouths stopped with these words thus by the king vttered, and so departed their waies. The bishop being still deteined in prison, procured suit to be made to the pope for his deliuerance: but the pope, being truelie informed of the matter, and wiselie considering that the king had not taken the bishop preaching, but fighting, and kept him prisoner rather as a rough enimie, than as a peaceable prelat, would not be earnest with the king for his deliuerance, but rather reprooued the bishop, in that he had preferred secular warfare before the spirituall, and had taken vpon him the [262]vse of a speare in stéed of a crosier, an helmet in steed of a miter, an herbergeon in stéed of a white rochet, a target for a stoale, and an iron sword in lieu of the spirituall sword: and therefore he refused to vse any commandement to king Richard for the setting of him at libertie. But yet he promised to doo what he could by waie of intreating that he might be released.

It is reported by some writers, that the pope at first, not vnderstanding the truth of the whole circumstance, should send to king Richard, commanding him by force of the canons of the church to deliuer his sons the bishop and archdeacon out of their captiuitie. To whom the king sent their armour with this message written in Latine, "Vide an *Genes. 37*.tunica filij tui sit an non," that is, "See whether these are the garments of thy sonnes or not:" alluding to the saieng of those that caried Josephs coate to Jacob. Which when the pope saw, he said: "Naie by S. Peter, it is neither the apparell of my sonnes, nor yet of my brethren: but rather they are the vestures of the children of Mars:" and so he left them still to be ransomed at the kings pleasure. The bishop thus séeing no hope to be deliuered without some agréement had betwixt the two kings, became now through irkesomenesse of his bonds, an earnest mediatour for peace, whereas before he had béene an extreme stirrer vp of war. Such a schoolemaister is imprisonment, & plucker downe of loftie courages. But to proceed.

An. Reg. 8.About the same time the archbishop of Rouen put all the countrie of Normandie vnder sentence of interdiction, bicause king Richard had begun Normandie interdicted by ye archbishop of Rouen.to fortifie a castell at Lisle Dandelie, vpon a péece of ground which the archbishop claimed to apperteine vnto his sée. The matter was brought before the pope, who perceiuing the intent of king Richard was not otherwise grounded vpon any couetous purpose to defraud the church of hir right, but onelie to build a fortresse in such place as was most expedient for defense of the countrie about, to preserue it from inuasion of the enimies; he counselled the archbishop not to stand against the king in it, but to exchange with him for some other lands: which was doone, and the interdiction by the pope released. The bishop The bishop of Elie departed this life.of Elie lord chancellour, being sent about this businesse towards Rome, departed this life by the way at Poictiers, in Januarie.

But the bishops of Durham & Lisieux that were sent with him, passed forward, and comming to Rome, informed the pope of the matter, who tooke order with the bishops (as before is mentioned.) The king gaue to the church in Rouen in recompense, his milles which he had in Rouen, so that the said church should paie the almes of old time appointed to be giuen for the same. He gaue to the said church likewise the towne of Diepe, and the towne of Bussels, so that the church should likewise paie the almes assigned foorth of the same, being the summe of 372 pounds of Aniouine monie: also the manour of Louers, and the forrest of Alermound with the deere and the appurtenances. But now to other dooings.

About the same time, or not long before, whereas there had béene long *Rog. Houed.* The king and the earle of Tholouse agréed.contention betwixt the kings of England, and the earles of S. Giles for the earldome of Tholouse, king Richard by way of aliance fell now at an appointment with the earle Raimond that held those lands; for whereas the countesse Constance wife to the said Raimond earle of Tholouse and aunt to king Philip was now departed this life, king Richard concluded a mariage betweene the said earle and his sister Joane quéene of Sicile, sometime wife to William king of Sicile, so that being thus ioined in aliance with the said earle of Tholouse on the one side, he procured a *Matt. Paris.* The earle of Flanders alied with K. Richard. *Iacob. Meir. Les annales de France.*league also with Baldwine earle of Flanders on the other, vnto whom he gaue fiue thousand markes in reward, vpon condition, that he should couenant not to grow to any agréement with the French king without his consent. Likewise Reginold the earle of Bolongne, that was sonne to earle of Chateau Marline, alied himselfe with them against the French king, and so did Baldwine earle of Guines with diuerse other.

Thus King Richard by such aliance hauing his part greatlie strengthened, prepared [263]himselfe to the warre more earnestlie than before, and tooke order with the earle of Flanders, that they should inuade the French dominions in two seuerall quarters both at one time, as the earle by Flanders, & he himselfe by Normandie, according to the appointment *Iacob. Meir. Wil. Paruus.*Towns won by the earle of Flanders.betwixt them deuised. The earle preparing an armie, first wan the towne of Dowaie, and then besieged saint Omers, and wan it after fiue weekes siege: wherevpon they of Aire yeelded to him; shortlie after he entred into Artois, & besieged the citie of Arras.

At the same time king Richard marching towards Gisors, wan in his waie Gisors besieged.the castell of Corselles, & destroied it; that doone, he came to Gisors, and besieged the towne, wasting all the countrie round about him where he came. The French king being thus troubled with the inuasion of his enimies in two seuerall places at one present time, sent certeine bands of his souldiors towards Arras to kéepe the earle of Flanders plaie, whilest he himselfe went against king Richard: and comming vnto Gisors, found it streictlie besieged of the same king, so that he wist not well how to enter the towne. But yet at length faigning to giue battell to king Richard (who vpon desire to receiue it, came abroad into the field) the French king rushed foorth with all his whole force to make towards The French king entreth into Gisors.the towne, & so got into it, though not without great losse and damage of his people.

King Richard not meaning to breake vp his siege from before the towne, (notwithstanding the French king had entred it) staied a certeine time of purpose to win it, knowing the gaine to be the greater, and his name more famous, if he might atchiue his purpose, now that his aduersarie K. Richard raiseth his siege.was within it, but when he saw it would not be, he raised his siege, and departed towards Cleremont, spoiling all the countrie by his forrais as he went, so that he wan great pillage, wherewith his souldiers were loden and made verie rich.

Hugh de Cheaumount taken prisoner.It chanced, that in a skirmish Hugh de Chaumount was taken prisoner, one that was of the French kings priuie councell; and king Richard appointed him to the kéeping of Robert Ros, who charged one of his seruants named William de Spinie with the custodie of him. But the said Hugh corrupting his kéeper the foresaid William with rewards, (whereof it is said,

Ouid. in 3. Art. am. ep. 16.——— acceptissima semperMunera sunt, author quæ pretiosa facit)

Robert Rosse put to his fine for an escape.escaped out of the castell of Bonneuille, where he was within ward, to the great displeasure of king Richard, who caused Robert Ros to paie for a fine, the summe of twelue hundred marks, which the prisoner should haue paied for his ransome: and further, commanded William de Spinie to be hanged for his disloiall dealing.

King Philip, after that the king of England was remooued from Gisors (as before yée haue heard) assembled a great host, and with banner *Matth. Paris.*displaied, entred into Normandie, and wasted the countrie from Newburge to Beaumont le Rogier, and that doone, returned into France, licencing *Nic. Treuet.* The French kings request for a combat.his men to returne vnto their homes. About the same time, he sent vnto king Richard, requiring him to appoint fiue champions, and he would appoint other fiue for his part, which might fight in lists, for triall of all matters in controuersie betwixt them, so to auoid the shedding of K. Richards answer.more giltlesse bloud. King Richard accepted the offer, with condition, that either king might be of the number, that is, the French king one of the fiue vpon the French part; & K. Richard one of the fiue vpon the English part. But this condition would not be granted. Herevpon when 1197.shortlie after it was signified to king Richard, that ships vsed to come *Matth. Paris.*out of England to saint Valerie with victuals, which were sold and conueied awaie vnto the French K and other his enimies, he rode to saint Valeries, and set the towne on fire, and such ships of England as he Ships burnt, and mariners

57

hanged.found there he also burnt, and hanged the mariners by the necke, diuiding the graine and other victuals which were found in the same ships amongst his owne souldiors.

[264]*Les annales de France.*About the same time he got the fauour of them of Champaigne and of the Britons, and William Crespine also was constreined to deliuer vnto him the castell of Auge, but the French king recouered it by siege, whilest king Richard entring into Aluergne wan diuerse castels there, to the An. Reg. 9.number of ten out of king Philips hands. In the meane time the earle of Flanders made sore war against the French king for his part, and training the same king within streits, so that he was almost inclosed on ech side, he constreined him to agrée to such composition as pleased the same earle to appoint, but afterwards the French king refused to stand to the couenants of that agréement, and so the warre continued betwixt them as before.

R. *Houed.* One yeare & 4 moneths saith *Wil. Paruus.*At length king Richard and the French king concluded vpon an abstinence of warre to indure from the feast of S. Hilarie for one whole yere, purposing in the meane time to make a finall peace and agréement. In which season Baldwine earle of Flanders came into England to doo his deuotions vnto the shrine where Thomas the archbishop laie buried at Canturburie. The same yeare also somewhat before this time, Rise ap Griffin king of Wales departed this life.Griffin king of Wales departed this life, after whose death there fell discord betwixt his sonnes for the succession, till the archbishop Hubert went to the marshes of that countrie and made an agréement betwixt them. Not long after, Roger the brother of Robert earle of Leicester, elected bishop of saint Andrews in Scotland, receiued the order of préesthood, and was consecrated bishop by the hands of the bishop of Aberdine.

Weights and measures.This yeare it was ordeined that measures of all manner of graine should conteine one quantitie throughout the realme, that is to saie, one resonable horsselode, and that the measures of wine and ale with all maner of liquors should be of one iust quantie according to the diuersitie of the liquor: also that weights should be of like rate throughout the relme, and that cloth should conteine two yards in breadth within the lists, of perfect goodnesse throughout, as well in the middest as by the sides, and that one manner of yard should be vsed through the relme. It was also ordeined that no merchants within the realme should hang any red or blacke clothes before their windowes, nor set vp any pentises or other thing whereby to darken the light from those that came to buy their cloth, so as they might be deceiued in choosing thereof.

Also it was enacted that there should be foure or six substantiall honest men chosen in euerie towne, and likewise in shires, with the head officers of cities and boroughes, which had a corporation, to see that the assises aforesaid were truelie kept, and that if anie were found to be offending in the premisses, to cause their bodies to be attached and commited to prison, and their goods to be seized to the kings vse: and if those that were chosen to haue regard thereto, were tried to be negligent, so that by others, and not by them any offenders chanced to be conuicted before the iustices, then should the regarders be put to their fines, for the negligent looking to their offices.

King Richard held his Christmasse this yeare at Roan, and Hubert the 1198.archbishop of Canturburie legat of the apostolike sée, named lord chéefe Justice of England, was about the same time in the marshes of Wales at Hereford, and there receiued into his hands the castels of Hereford, Bridgenorth and Ludlow, remoouing those that had the same in kéeping, and appointing others in their roomes. Afterwards comming by Couentrie, Moonks placed againe in the church of Couentrie.he placed the moonks againe in the cathedrall church of that citie, by commandement of pope Celestine, and chased out the secular canons, which the bishop Hugh Nouant had brought into the same church when he remooued the moonks.

Messengers from the stats of Germanie.In the Christmasse wéeke also there came messengers to Rouen from the archbishops of Cullen and Mentz, and from other states of the empire, which declared vnto king Richard, that all the princes of Germanie were appointed to assemble at Cullen, the two & twentith of Februarie, about the choosing of a new emperour, in place of the late deceassed Henrie: and therefore they commanded him by force of the oth and league in which he was bound to the emperour and empire, that all excuse of deniall or occasions to the contrarie ceasing and set apart, he should make his

58

repaire vnto Cullen at the aforesaid day, to helpe them in choosing of some worthie personage that might and was [265]able to haue the empire. King Richard doubting to put himselfe in danger, bicause he had not discharged all the debts due for his ransome, staied at home, but yet he sent diuerse noble men thither, and did so much in fauour of his nephue Otho, that by the helpe of the foresaid two archbishops of Cullen and Mentz, the same Otho was elected emperour. But of this matter more shall be said hereafter.

Three hundred knights of men of armes to be found.Moreouer, about the same time king Richard required by the archbishop of Canturburie his chéefe iustice, an aid of 300 knights to be found by his subiects of England, to remaine with him in his seruice for one whole yeare, or else that they would giue him so much monie, as might serue to reteine that number after the rate of thrée shillings a daie of English monie for euerie knight. Whereas all other were contented to be The bishop of Lincolne.contributors herein, onelie Hugh bishop of Lincolne refused, and spake sore against the archbishop that moued the matter. But how soeuer that request tooke place, king Richard (as we find) leuied this yeare a subsidie of fiue shillings of euerie hide of land within the realme, two commissioners, that is to say, one of the spiritualtie, & a knight of the temporaltie, being appointed as commissioners in euerie shire, with the assistance of the shiriffe, and others, to sée the same assessed & rated after an hundred acres of land to the hide of land, according to the custome.

The moonks of Christes church send to the pope, complaining of their archbishop.The same yeare also the moonks of the house of the holie Trinitie, otherwise called Christes church in Canturburie, exhibited their complaint vnto pope Innocent, that their archbishop Hubert (contrarie to his order and dignitie) exercised the office of high iustice, and sate in iudgement of bloud, being so incumbred in temporall matters, that he could not haue time to discharge his office touching spirituall causes: The pope sendeth to the king.wherevpon the pope sent vnto king Richard, admonishing him not to suffer the said archbishop to be any longer troubled with temporall affaires, but to discharge him thereof, and not to admit any spirituall person from thencefoorth vnto any temporall administration.

He further prohibited by vertue of their obedience, all manner of prelats and men of the church, that they should not presume rashlie to take vpon them any maner of secular function or office. Whervpon the archbishop was discharged of his office of chéefe iustice, and Geffrey Fitz Peter succéeded in gouernement of the realme in his stéed. ¶ Geruasius Dorobernensis saith, that the archbishop resigned that office of his owne accord, and that not till after his returne from the marshes of Wales, where he had ouerthrowne the Welshmen, and slaine fiue thousand of them. Which victorie other ascribe vnto Geffrey Fitz Peter, which Geffrey (as the said Dorobernensis saith) succeeded the archbishop in the office of lord chéefe iustice, but not vntill August, in the tenth yeare of the kings reigne.

An. Reg. 10.In this yeare, immediatlie vpon the expiring of the truce which was taken till haruest might be ended, the warre betwixt the two kings of England & France began eftsoones to be pursued with like earnestnesse as before: wherevpon manie encounters chanced betwixt the parties, with taking of townes and fortresses, as commonlie in such cases it happeneth. Twise the French king was put to the worsse, once in September betwixt Gamages and Vernon, where he was driuen to saue himselfe by flight, loosing twentie knights, and thréescore seruitors or yomen, which were taken, besides those that were slaine: and againe, in the same moneth on Michaelmasse euen betwixt Curseilles and Gisors, at what time he came to succour Curseilles, bringing with him 400 knights, besides seruitors, and a great multitude of commons. But the castell was woone before he could approch it.

King Richard being aduertised of his comming, hasted foorth to méet him, and giuing the onset vpon him, forced him to flée vnto Gisors, where at the entring of the bridge there was such preasse, that the bridge brake, so that amongst other, the king himselfe with his horsse and all fell King Philip almost drowned.into the riuer of Geth, and with much adoo was releeued, and got out of the water, no small number of right hardie and valiant gentlemen being taken at the same time, which put themselues forward to staie the Englishmen, till the king was recouered [266]out of the present danger. To conclude, there were taken to the number of an hundred knights, and two Seuen score saith R. Houed.Matth. Paris. R. Houed.hundred barded horsses, besides seruitors on horssebacke, and footmen with crossebowes. Amongst other prisoners these are named,

Matthew de Montmorancie, Gales de Ports, Iollen de Bray, and manie other also innumerable. King Richard hauing got this victorie, wrote letters thereof vnto the archbishops, bishops, abbats, earles and barons of his realme, that they might praise God for his good successe.

¶ A notable example to all princes that haue the conquest ouer their enimies, to referre the happie getting thereof to God, and to giue praise vnto him who giueth victorie vnto whom it pleaseth him. Which the Psalmograph saw verie well, and therefore ascribed all the issue of his prosperous affaires to God, as may well be noted by his words, saieng expresselie,

Eob. Hess. in Psal. 144.——— ab illoMunior, hic instar turris & arcis erat,Dura manus in bella meas qui format & armat,Ad fera qui digitos instruit arma meos.

Now will we staie the proceedings of the king of France at this time, and make no further relation thereof for a while, till we haue touched other things that happened in England at the same season. And first ye shall vnderstand, that Hugh Bardolfe, Roger Arundell, and Geffrey Hachet, to whom as iustices, the counties of Lincolne, Notingham, Yorke, Derbie, Northumberland, Westmerland, Cumberland, and Lancaster were appointed for circuits, held not onelie plées of assises, and of the Inquisitions taken.crowne, but also tooke inquisitions of escheats, and forfaitures of all maner of transgressions, and of donations of benefices, of marriages of widowes and maids, and other such like things as apperteined to the king, whereby any aduantages grew to his vse, the which for tediousnesse we passe ouer. These things were streightlie looked vnto, not without the disquieting of manie.

Herewith came an other trouble in the necke of this former, to diuerse persons within the realme, through inquiries taken by the iustices of the forrests: for Hugh Neuille, Hugh Waley, and Heruisius Neuill, appointed iustices itinerants in that case, were commanded by the king to call before them archbishops, bishops, earles, barons, knights, and fréeholders, with the reeue, and foure of the substantiall men of euerie Ordinances of forrests.towne or village, to heare and take knowledge of the kings commandement, touching the ordinances of forrests, the which were verie straight in sundrie points, so that whereas before those that offended in killing of the kings deere were punished by the purse, now they should loose their eies and genitals, as the lawe was in the daies of king Henrie his grandfather: and those that offended in cutting downe woods or bushes, or in digging and deluing vp of turues and clods, or by any other maner of waie made waste and distruction in woods or grasse, or spoile of venison, within the precinct of the forrests, contrarie to order, they should be put to their fines.

Préests to be arrested offending in forrests.He gaue commandement also, that it should be lawful to the forresters to take and put vnder arrest, as well préests and those of the cleargie, as temporall men, being found offendors in forrest grounds and chases. Manie other ordinances were decréed touching the preseruation of forrests, and the kings prerogatiue, aduantages and profits rising and growing by the same, as well for sauing of his woods and wasts, as in pannage and agistements, greatlie to the restraint of them that might vsurpe or incroch vpon the grounds within the compasse of his forrests.

Ye haue heard before, how the moonks of Canturburie did send to exhibit a complaint to the pope, for that their archbishop tooke vpon him to *Ger. Dor.*deale in exercise of matters belonging to a temporall man, and not to such a one as had rule ouer the spiritualtie: but this was not the cause that did gréeue them so much, as that he went forward with the erection of that church at Lameth, which his predecessor archbishop Baldwine had first [267]begun at Haketon, now called S. Stephans (as before ye haue heard) and after was driuen through the importunate suit of the moonks to leaue off, and race that which he had there begun, to obeie the popes The church of Lameth.pleasure: and after laid a new foundation at Lameth.

The moonks of Canturburie therefore still fearing least that church should greatlie preiudice such rights and liberties, as they pretended, namlie in the election of their archbishop, would neuer rest, but still complained and followed their suit in most obstinate maner in the court of Rome, as well in the daies of the said Baldwine, as now against Hubert, (when he tooke in hand to continue the worke according to the purpose of his predecessour the said Baldwine, which was to haue instituted a colledge there, and to haue placed secular canons in the same) and such was the earnest trauell of the moonks herein, that in the end now after the deceasse of pope Celestine, they found such fauour at the hands of pope Innocent his successor, that the same Innocent The pope cōmandeth the church of Lameth to be raced.directed his letters of cōmandement to the archbishop, and other bishops of this land, to destroie and race the same foundation, as a péece of worke derogatorie to the sée of Canturburie, and verie preiudiciall to the estate of holie church.

The archbishop at the first trusted to be borne out by the king (who was highlie offended with the moonks for their presumptuous dealing) and therefore refused to obeie the popes commandement. The king in deed stomached the matter so highlie, that he sent letters vnto the moonks by no worsse messengers than by Geffrey Fitz Peter, and Hugh Fitz Bardolfe his iustices, signifieng to them not onelie his high displeasure for their presumptuous proceedings in their suit without his consent, but also commanding them to surceasse, and not to procéed further in the matter by virtue of any such the popes letters, which they had purchased contrarie to the honour and dignitie of his crowne and realme. Moreouer, he wrote to the bishops, commanding them to appeale; and to the archbishop, forbidding him in any wise to breake downe the church which he had so builded at Lameth.

The shiriffe of Kent also was commanded to seize into his hands all the The presumtuous stoutnesse of the moonks.tenements and possessions that belonged to the moonks (a frie of satan and as one saith verie well of them and the like leuen of lewdnesse,

—— sentina malorum,Agnorum sub pelle lupi, mercede colentesNon pietate Deum, &c.)

who neuer the lesse were so stout in that quarell, that they would not prolong one daie of the time appointed by the pope for the racing of that church. Herevpon the king for his part and the bishops in their owne behalfes wrote to the pope. Likewise the abbats of Boxeley, Fourd, Stratford, Roberts-bridge, Stanlie, and Basing Warke, wrote the matter to him: and againe the pope and the cardinals wrote to the king, to the archbishops, and bishops: and so letters passed to and fro, till at length the pope sent a Nuncio of purpose, to signifie his full determination, as in the next yeare it shall be shewed at full.

Welshmen vanquished.*Ger. Dor.* ascribeth this victorie vnto Hubert archb. of Canturburie and saith there were slaine about 500 of the enimies. Mauds castle.About the same time Geffrey Fitz Peter, lord cheefe iustice of England, raised a power of men, and went into Wales to succour the tenants of William de Brause, which were besieged of the king, or rather prince of that countrie, named Owen, the brother of Cadwalaine, in Mauds castell: but the lord chéefe iustice comming to the reskue of them within, gaue battell to the aduersaries, and vanquishing them slue three thousand of them, and seauen hundred of those that were taken prisoners and wounded. And all the while the warres continued in France, the losse for the most part still redounded to the Frenchmen. Earle John burnt Newburg, and tooke eighteene knights of such as were sent to the reskue.

The earle of Leicester.The earle of Leicester with a small companie came before the castell of Pascie, which (although the Frenchmen held it) did yet of right belong vnto the said earle. The souldiors within issued foorth, and being too strong for the earle, caused him to flee, for otherwise [268]he had béene taken. But returning on the morrow after with more companie about him, and laieng ambushes for the enimie, he approched the said castell, and trained the Frenchmen foorth till he had them within his danger, and then causing his men to breake out vpon them tooke an eighteene knights, Marchades.and a great multitude of other people. Also Marchades with his rout of Brabanders did the Frenchmen much hurt, in robbing and spoiling the countries.

About this season the archbishop of Canturburie went ouer into Normandie to speake with king Richard, and at the French kings request he passed into France, to common with him of peace, which the French king offered to conclude, in restoring all the townes and castels which he had taken (Gisors onelie excepted) and touching the possession and title thereof, he was contented to put the matter in compremise, to the order and award of six barons in Normandie to be named by him; and of six barons in France which king Richard should name. But king Richard would not thus agrée, except the earle of Flanders and others which had forsaken the French king to take his part, might be comprised in the same peace. At length yet in Nouember, there was truce taken betwixt the two kings till the feast of S. Hilarie next insuing.

In the meane time pope Innocent the third, vnderstanding in what present danger things stood in the holie land, and on the other side, A truce taken betwixt the two kings.considering what a weakening it was vnto christendome, to haue these two kings thus to warre with mortall hatred one against the other: he thought it stood him vpon to trauell betwixt them, to bring them vnto some peace and agreement. Héerevpon he dispatched one Peter the cardinall of Capua into France, as legat from the sée of Rome, vnto the two foresaid kings, to instruct them in what present danger the state of the christians in Asia presentlie stood, so that without the aid of them and of other christian princes, it could not be holpen, but needs it must come to vtter ruine, and the Saracens yer long to be possessed of the whole. Therefore both in respect hereof, and also for the auoiding of the further wilfull spilling of christian bloud in such ciuill[17] and vngodlie warre, he besought them to staie their hands, and to ioine in some fréendlie band of concord, whereby they might with mutuall consent bestow their seruice in that necessarie and most godlie warre, wherein by ouercomming the enimies of Christ, they might looke for worthie reward at his hands, which is the frée giuer of all victories.[18]

1199.The cardinall comming into France, and dooing his message in most earnest wise, was present at the interuiew appointed betwixt the two kings in the feast of S. Hilarie, but yet could not he bring his purpose R. *Houed.* A truce concluded for fiue yeares.to full effect: onelie he procured them to take truce for the term of fiue yeares, farther he could not get them to agrée. ¶ The fault by authors is ascribed aswell to king Richard, as to king Philip: for king Richard being first euill vsed, and put to hinderance, determined either to vanquish, or neuer to giue place.

This forbearance from warre was concluded and taken in the yeare 1199 after the incarnation, and tenth of king Richards reigne. But immediatlie after, there arose matter of new displeasure betwixt these two kings to kéepe their minds in vre with secret grudges, though by reason of the truce they outwardlie absteined from declaring it by force Contention about the choosing of the emperour.of armes. It chanced that in the election of a new emperour, the electors could not agrée, one part of them choosing Otho duke of Saxonie, nephue to king Richard by his sister Maud, and another part of them naming Philip duke of Tuscaine, and brother to the last emperour Henrie.

King Richard (as reason was) did procure what fauour he could to the furtherance of his nephue Otho: and king Philip on the contrarie part, did what he could in fauour of the foresaid Philip. At length Otho was admitted by the pope to end the strife: but yet the grudge remained in the harts of the two kings: Philip finding himselfe much gréeued in that he had missed his purpose, and Richard being as little pleased for [269]that he had woone his so hardlie, and with so much adoo. And thus matters passed for that yeare.

R. *Houed.* The popes letters to the king for the church of Lameth.In the beginning of the next, the popes Nuncio came with letters, not onlie to the archbishop and bishops of England, but also to the king himselfe, signifieng the popes resolute decree touching the church and colledge of Lameth to be broken downe and suppressed. Wherevpon the king and archbishop (though sore against their willes) when they saw no waie longer to shift off the matter, yéelded to the popes pleasure: and so the archbishop sent his letters to Lameth, where the 21 daie of Januarie they were read, and the 27 daie of the same moneth was the church cast downe, & the canons which were alreadie these placed, had commandement to depart from thence without further delaie. Thus the moonks in dispite The moonks borne out by the pope.of the king and archbishop had their willes, but yet their vexation ceassed not, for the king and archbishop bearing them no small euill will, for that they had so obteined their purpose contrarie to their minds and intents, molested them diuerse waies, although the moonks still vpon complaint to the pope, were verie much reléeued, and found great fréendship both with him and likewise with his court. ¶ So that it may be obserued that these dishclouts of the popes kitchen haue in all ages, since their first quickening béene troublesome and mutinous, sawcie and insolent, proud[19] and malapert. But,

*M. Pal. in suo sag.*Proh pudor! hos tolerare potest ecclesia porcos,Cùm sint lasciui nimiùm, nimiúmq; superbi,Duntaxàt ventri, veneri somnóq; vacantes?

In this meane time, king Richard being now at rest from troubles of warre, studied busilie to prouide monie, meaning to make a new voiage into the holie land. Therefore finding himselfe beare of treasure, by A tax. Fiue shillings of euerie plough land, as saith*Matt. Westm.* Chasteau Galiard built.reason of the French warres had emptied his cofers, he set a great tax vpon his subiects, and by that meanes, hauing recouered a great summe, he builded that notable strong castell in Normandie, vpon the banke of the riuer of Saine, named Chateau Galiard: which when it was finished he fell a iesting thereat and said; "Behold, is not this a faire daughter of one yeares growth." The soile where this castell was builded, belonged to the archbishop of Rouen, for which there followed great strife betwixt the king and the archbishop, till the pope tooke vp the matter (as before ye haue heard.)

After this, he determined to chastise certeine persons in Poictou, which during the warres betwixt him and the French king, had aided the Images of an emperour and of his wife & children all of fine gold. The annales of Aquitaine.Frenchmen against him: wherevpon with an armie he passed foorth towards them, but by the waie he was informed, that one Widomer a vicount in the countrie of Britaine, had found great treasure: and therefore pretending a right thereto by vertue of his prerogatiue, he sent for the vicount, who smelling out the matter, and supposing the king would not be indifferent in parting the treasure, fled into Limosin, where although the people were tributaries to the king of England, yet they tooke part with the French king.

Chalus Cheuerell.*R. Houed.*There is a towne in that countrie called Chalus Cheuerell, into which the said vicount retired for safegard of himselfe, and then gaue the townesmen a great portion of treasure, to the end they should defend him and his quarell for the rest. King Richard still following him, as one that could not auoid his fatall ordinance, hasted into the confines of Limosin, fullie determining either to win the towne by force, if the inhabitants should make resistance, or at leastwise, to get into his hands the preie, which he so earnestlie pursued. At his first approch he K. Richard besiegeth Chalus.gaue manie fierce assaults to the towne, but they within hauing throughlie prouided aforehand for to defend a siege, so resisted his attempts, that within thrée daies after his comming, he ceassed to assaile the towne, meaning to vndermine the walles, which otherwise he perceiued would verie hardlie be gotten; considering the stoutnesse of them within, and withall, the naturall strength and situation of the place it selfe.

Herevpon therefore on the 26 of March, whiles he (togither with capteine Marchades) [270]went about vnaduisedlie to view the towne (the better to consider the place which waie he might conueie the course of his mine) He is wounded.they came so farre within danger, that the king was stricken in the left arme, or (as some write) in the shoulder, where it ioined to the necke, with a quarell inuenomed (as is to be supposed by the sequele.) Being *Ra. Niger.*thus wounded, he gat to his horsse, and rode home againe to his lodging, where he caused the wound to be searched and bound vp, and as a man nothing dismaid therewith, continued his siege with such force and assurance, that within 12 daies after the mishap, the towne was yéelded vnto him, although verie little treasure (to make any great accompt of) was at that time found therein.

In this meane season, the king had committed the cure of his wound to one of Marchades his surgions, who taking in hand to plucke out the quarell, drew foorth onelie the shaft at the first[20], and left the iron still within, and afterwards going about most vnskilfullie to get foorth the head of the said quarell, he vsed such incisions, and so mangled the The king despaired of life.kings arme, yer he could cut it, that he himself despaired of all helpe and longer life, affirming flatlie to such as stood about him, that he could not long continue by reason of his butcherlie handling. To be short féeling himselfe to wax weaker and weaker, preparing his mind to death, which he perceiued now to be at hand, he ordeined his testament, He ordeineth his testament.or rather reformed and added sundrie things vnto the same which he before had made, at the time of his gooing foorth towards the holie land.

Vnto his brother Iohn he assigned the crowne of England, and all other his lands and dominions, causing the Nobles there present to sweare fealtie vnto him. His monie, his iewels, and all other his goods R. *Houed.*mooueable he willed to be diuided into thrée parts, of the which Otho the emperor his sisters sonne to haue one, his houshold seruants an other part, and the third to be distributed to the poore. Finallie remembring himselfe also of the place of his buriall, he commanded that his bodie should be interred at Fonteurard at his fathers feet, but the *Matth. Paris.*willed his heart to be conueied vnto Rouen, and there buried, in testimonie of the loue which he had euer borne vnto that citie for the stedfast faith and tried loialtie at all times found in the citizens there. His bowels he ordeined to be buried in Poictiers, as in a place naturallie vnthankefull and not worthie to reteine any of the more honorable parts of his bodie.

Moreouer he caused the arcubalistar that wounded him, to be sought out, whose name was Barthram de Garden[21], or Peter Basill (for so he named himselfe as some write) who being brought before the king, he demanded *Rog. Houed.*wherein he had so much offended him, that he should so lie in wait to slea him, rather than Marchades, who was then in his companie, and attendant on his person? The other answered boldlie againe, saieng; "I purposed to kill thee, bicause thou sluest my father, and two of my brethren heretofore, and wouldest also now haue slaine me, if I had happened to fall into thy hands. Wherefore I intended to reuenge their deaths, not caring in the meane time what became of my selfe, so that I might in anie wise obteine my will of thée, who in such sort hast bereft me of my freends." The king harkening vnto his words, and pondering his A notable example of forgiuing an enimie.*Matth. Paris.*talke by good aduisement, fréelie pardoned him, and withall commanded that he should be set at libertie, and thereto haue an hundred shillings giuen him in his pursse, and so to be let go. Moreouer, he gaue strait charge that no[22] man should hurt him, or séeke any reuenge for this his death hereafter. Thus the penitent prince not onelie forgaue, but also rewarded his aduersarie. Howbeit after his deceasse, Marchades getting him into his hands, first caused the skin to be stripped off his bodie, and after hanged him on a gibit.

King Richard departed this life.At length king Richard by force of sicknesse (increased with anguish of his incurable wound) departed this life, on the tuesdaie before Palmesundaie, being the ninth of Aprill, and the xj. daie after he was hurt, in the yeare after the birth of our Sauiour 1199. in the 44 yeare of his age, and after he had reigned nine yeares, nine moneths, and od His stature & shape of bodie. *Gal. Vinsaf.*daies: he left no issue behind him. He was tall of stature, and well proportioned, faire and comelie of face, so as in his countenance appeared much fauour and grauitie, of haire [271]bright aborne, as it were betwixt red and yellow, with long armes, and nimble in all his ioints his thighes and legs were of due proportion, and answerable to the other parts of his bodie.

His disposition of mind.As he was comelie of personage, so was he of stomach more couragious and fierce, so that not without cause, he obteined the surname of Cueur de lion, that is to saie, The lions hart. Moreouer he was courteous to his souldiors, and towards his fréends and strangers that resorted vnto him verie liberall, but to his enimies hard and not to be intreated, desirous of battell, an enimie to rest and quietnesse, verie eloquent of speech and wise, but readie to enter into ieopardies, and that without feare or forecast in time of greatest perils.

The vices that were in king Richard.These were his vertuous qualities, but his vices (if his vertues, his age, and the wars which he mainteined were throughlie weied) were either none at all, or else few in number, and not verie notorious. He was noted of the common people to be partlie subiect vnto pride, which surelie for the most part foloweth stoutnesse of mind: of incontinencie, to the which his youth might happilie be somewhat bent: and of couetousnesse, into the which infamie most capticins and such princes as commonlie follow the warres doo oftentimes fall, when of the necessitie they are driuen to exact monie, as well of fréends as enimies, to mainteine the infinit charges of their wars.

Hereof it came, that on a time whiles he soiourned in France about his warres, which he held against K. Philip, there came vnto him a French Fulco a préest.préest whose name was Fulco, who required the K. in any wise to put from him thrée abhominable daughters which he had, and to bestow them in marriage, least God punished him for them. Thou liest hypocrite (said the king) to thy verie face, for all the world knoweth that I haue not one daughter. I lie not (said the préest) for thou hast thrée daughters, one of them is called pride, the second couetousnesse, and the third lecherie. With that the king, called to him his lords & barons, and said to them; "This hypocrite heere hath required me to marrie awaie my thrée daughters, which (as he saith) I cherish, nourish, foster and maintcine, that is to say pride, couetousnesse, and lecherie. And now that I haue found out necessarie & fit husbands for them, I will doo it with effect, and seeke no more delaies. I therefore bequeath my pride to the high minded templers and hospitallers, which are as proud as Lucifer himselfe. My couetousnesse I giue vnto the white moonks, otherwise called of the Cisteaux order, for they couet the diuell and all. My lecherie I commit to the prelates of the church, who haue most pleasure and felicitie therein."

Baldwine & Hubert archbishops of Canturburie. There liued in the daies of this king Richard, men of worthie fame amongst those of the cleargie, Baldwine archbishop of Canturburie, and Hubert who succeeded him in that sée, also Hugh bishop of Lincolne, a man for his worthinesse of life highlie to be commended. Moreouer, William bishop of Elie, who though otherwise he was to be dispraised for his ambition and pompous hautinesse, yet the king vsed his seruice for a time greatlie to his profit and aduancement of the publike affaires. Also of learned men we find diuerse in these daies that flourished here in this land, as Baldwine of Deuonshire that came to the bishop of Worcester in this kings time, and after his deceasse, he was aduanced to the gouernment of the archbishops sée of Canturburie, who wrote diuerse *Iohn Bales*.treatises, namelie of matters perteining to diuinitie. Daniell Morley well seene in the Mathematicals, Iohn de Hexam, and Richard de Hexham two notable historians; Guilielmus Stephanides a moonke of Canturburie, who wrote much in the praise of archbishop Becket. Beside these, we find one Richard, that was an abbat of the order Premonstratensis, Richard Diuisiensis, Nicholas Walkington, Robert de Bello Foco, an excellent philosopher, &c. ¶ See Bale in his third Centurie.

In martiall renowme there flourished in this kings daies diuerse noble capteines, as Robert earle of Leicester, Ranulfe de Fulgiers, two of the Bardulphes, Hugh and Henrie, thrée Williams, Marshall, Brunell, and Mandeuill, with two Roberts, Ros and Sabeuile. Furthermore, I find that A great derth.in the daies of this king Richard, a great derth reigned in England, [272]and also in France, for the space of three or foure yeares during the wars betwéene him & king Philip, so that after his returne out of Germanie, and from imprisonment, a quarter of wheat was sold at 18 shillings eight pence, no small price in those daies, if you consider the alay of monie then currant.

Also immediatlie after, that is to say, in the yeare of our Lord, a thousand, one hundred, nintie six, which was about the seuenth yere of A great mortalitie of people. *Wil. Paruus*.the said kings reigne, there followed a maruellous sore death, which dailie consumed such numbers of people, that scarse there might be found any to kéepe and looke to those that were sicke, or to burie them that died. Which sickenesse was a pestilentiall feuer or sharpe burning ague. The accustomed manner of buriall was also neglected: so that in manie places they made great pits, and threw their dead bodies into the same, one vpon an other. For the multitude of them that died was such, that they could not haue time to make for euerie one a seuerall graue. This mortalitie continued for the space of fiue or six months, and at length ceassed in the cold season of winter.

Two sunnes.In the octaues of Pentecost before this great death, in the first houre of the day, there appeared two sunnes, the true sunne & another, as it were a counterfeit sunne: but so apparentlie, that hard it was to the common people, to discerne the one from the other. The skilfull also were compelled by instruments to distinguish the one from the other: in taking their altitudes and places, whereby in the end they found the new apparition, as it were, to wait vpon the planet, and so continued by the space of certeine houres. At length when the beholders (of whom Wil. Paruus that recorded things in that age was one) had well wearied their eies in diligent marking the maner of this strange appearance, the counterfeit sunne vanished awaie.

¶ This strange woonder was taken for a signification of that which followed, that is to say, of war, famine and pestilence: or to say the truth, it betokened rather the continuance of two of those mischiefs. For warre and famine had sore afflicted the people before that time, and as yet ceassed not: but as for the pestilence, it began soone after the strange sight, whereof insued such effect, as I haue alreadie rehearsed.

Thus farre king Richard.

Printed in Great Britain
by Amazon